BLACK PANTHER

MARVEL

First published in 2023 by Epic Ink, an imprint of The Quarto Group,
142 West 36th Street, 4th Floor, New York, NY 10018, USA
T (212) 779-4972 F (212) 779-6058 www.Quarto.com

Epic Ink titles are also available at discount for retail, wholesale, promotional, and bulk purchase. For details, contact the Special Sales Manager by email at specialsales@quarto.com or by mail at The Quarto Group, Attn: Special Sales Manager, 100 Cummings Center Suite 265D, Beverly, MA 01915 USA.

10 9 8 7 6 5 4 3 2 1

ISBN: 978-0-7603-7561-7

Library of Congress Cataloging-in-Publication Data

Names: Womack, Ytasha, author.
Title: Black Panther, a cultural exploration / by Ytasha Womack.
Description: New York, NY : Epic Ink, 2023. | Includes bibliographical
    references and index. | Summary: "Black Panther: A Cultural Exploration
    charts the compelling people and times that contributed to the comic's
    evolution, from the 1960s to today"-- Provided by publisher.
Identifiers: LCCN 2023005024 (print) | LCCN 2023005025 (ebook) | ISBN
    9780760375617 (hardcover) | ISBN 9780760375624 (ebook)
Subjects: LCSH: Black Panther (Fictitious character) | Black Panther
    (Motion picture : 2018) | Comic books, strips, etc.--United
    States--History. | Marvel Comics Group--History. | Superheroes, Black. |
    Afrofuturism.
Classification: LCC PN6728.B519338 W66 2023 (print) | LCC PN6728.B519338
    (ebook) | DDC 741.5/973--dc23/eng/20230203
LC record available at https://lccn.loc.gov/2023005024
LC ebook record available at https://lccn.loc.gov/2023005025

Group Publisher: Rage Kindelsperger
Creative Director: Laura Drew
Managing Editor: Cara Donaldson
Editor: Katie McGuire
Cover and Interior Design: Scott Richardson

Printed in China

Authentic
PORTUGUESE
COOKING

More Than 185 Classic Mediterranean-Style Recipes of the Azores, Madeira and Continental Portugal

Ana Patuleia Ortins

creator of Portuguesecooking.com and author of *Portuguese Homestyle Cooking*

YTASHA L. WOMACK

BLACK PANTHER
A CULTURAL EXPLORATION

EPIC INK

Black Panther artwork by Esad Ribic

This book is for all the Black Panther
fans who've read the comics over
the years and continue to give
life to this brilliant character.

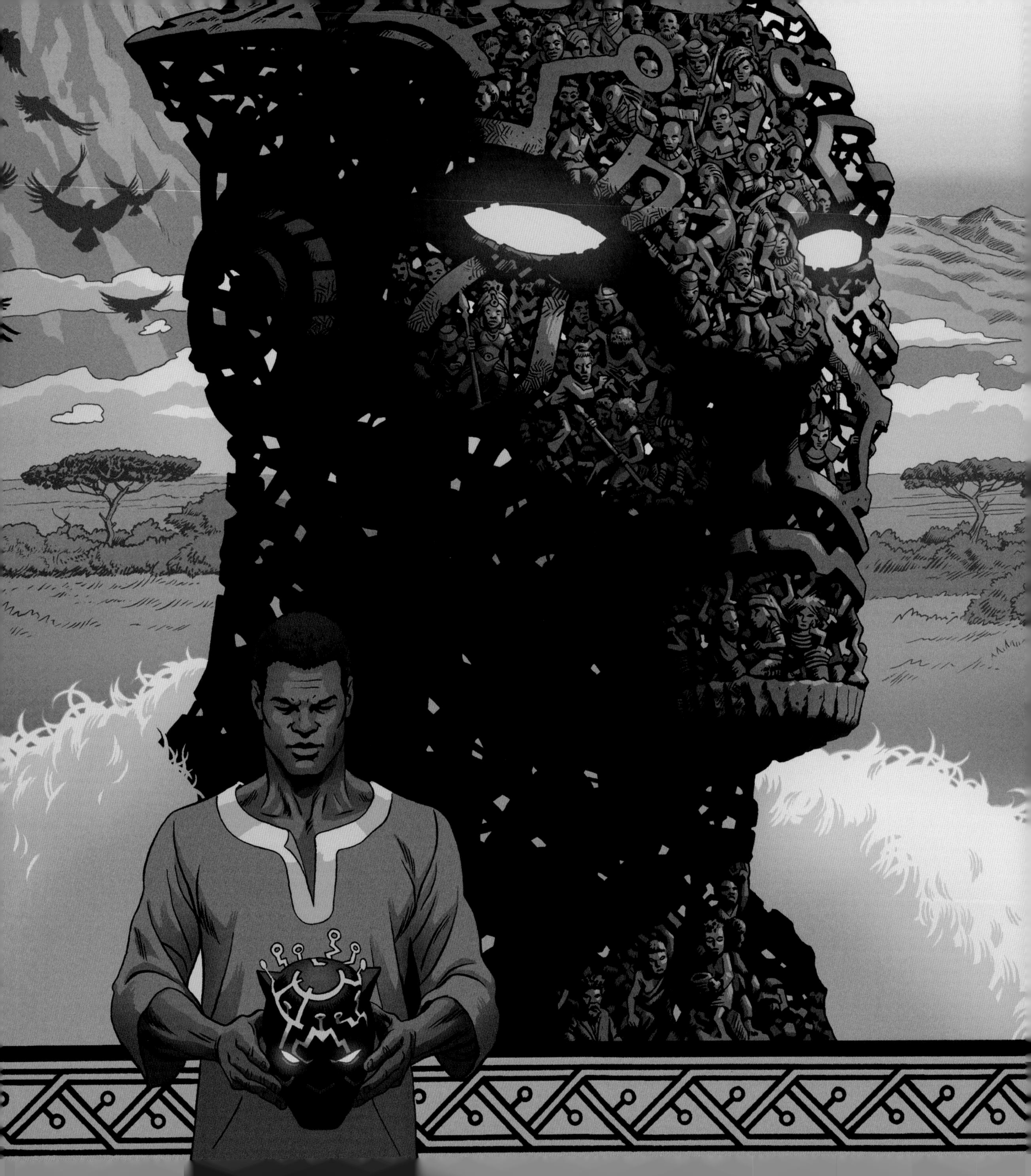

CONTENTS

INTRODUCTION

"I am the Panther King who stalks the soul across ocean, desert, and plane."
—T'Challa (*A Nation Under Our Feet*, Book 2)

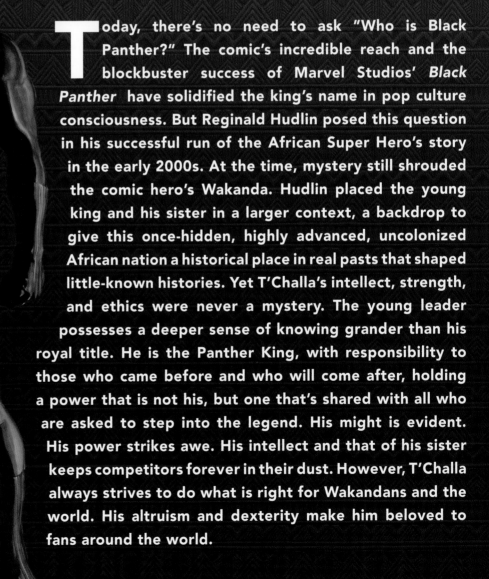

Today, there's no need to ask "Who is Black Panther?" The comic's incredible reach and the blockbuster success of Marvel Studios' *Black Panther* have solidified the king's name in pop culture consciousness. But Reginald Hudlin posed this question in his successful run of the African Super Hero's story in the early 2000s. At the time, mystery still shrouded the comic hero's Wakanda. Hudlin placed the young king and his sister in a larger context, a backdrop to give this once-hidden, highly advanced, uncolonized African nation a historical place in real pasts that shaped little-known histories. Yet T'Challa's intellect, strength, and ethics were never a mystery. The young leader possesses a deeper sense of knowing grander than his royal title. He is the Panther King, with responsibility to those who came before and who will come after, holding a power that is not his, but one that's shared with all who are asked to step into the legend. His might is evident. His power strikes awe. His intellect and that of his sister keeps competitors forever in their dust. However, T'Challa always strives to do what is right for Wakandans and the world. His altruism and dexterity make him beloved to fans around the world.

Akili: "Power is all you've ever known. So what would you do to hold onto it? Create a crisis from which only 'Black Panther' can save us?"

T'Challa: "You paint the picture of a crazed dictator. I have always been a people's king."

—Black Panther: *The Long Shadow*, Part 3

We are some years beyond the once-asked question of whether a Black super hero could attract legions of fans. Comedic legend Richard Pryor joked in his 1977 comedy album *Who Me? I'm Not Him* that he always wanted to see a Black super hero, but expected that Hollywood would create one riddled with all the stereotypes of the

day. Just as some people thought they'd never see a Black president, there were many more who thought they'd never see a respectfully created Black super hero in mainstream comics or film.

Black Panther's success squashed those fears. The blossoming world of comic heroes of color new and old, often brought to life by creators of color, is evidence of that. In one sense, Black Panther is the little comic that could, a train driving up a steep hill of skepticism about what a Black super hero could do in the public forum—for that matter, what Black people could do, as well. In time,

Chadwick Boseman attends the European premiere of *Black Panther* (2018) in London on February 8, 2018.

Richard Pryor performing at Cafe Wha? in Greenwich Village, 1964.

this comic would gain traction, morphing into a bullet train of success, with a solo film, multiple appearances in the Marvel Cinematic Universe, and a massive fan base around the world.

"The Black Panther being who he is isn't a new thing," said Darryl "DMC" McDaniels of the legendary hip-hop group Run-DMC in an interview with *Double Down News*. "We just needed to let the world know he existed."

"I am T'Challa," rapped Kendrick Lamar in the song named for the king. The cultural connection to Wakanda's leader runs deep. Black Panther's very existence means a great deal to fans and nonfans alike. And today's far reach of the Black Panther tale lends itself to other questions: If Black Panther lives in hearts and minds, then who am I? If Wakanda is forever, then who are we?

Black Panther is a living, breathing mythos—a modern myth informed by liberation struggles, histories, the otherworldly, and aspirations. Black Panther reshapes consciousness. His story is both an amalgamation of wished-upon dreams and an inspiration for those dreams. A tapestry of culture and hope is pushed forward with every page drawn of T'Challa's adventures.

At its core, Black Panther is the tale of a young, promising prince who abruptly becomes king after his father's murder. T'Challa's father, King T'Chaka, was murdered by the vengeful despot Ulysses S. Klaw. In the aftermath, T'Challa must juggle the usual demands of life—family, friends, romantic relationships— and the legacy of the Black Panther cult with leading a revered nation whose technological and mystical prowess is a sought-after curiosity and perceived threat.

of Wakanda's place in the world, and Wakandans expect nothing less than sheer brilliance.

T'Challa's mother, a scientist named N'Yami, passed away while giving birth to him, something with which he has never quite reconciled. His stepmother, Queen Ramonda, a woman born beyond Wakanda's borders, is a staunch supporter as T'Challa rules. Shuri, T'Challa's younger sister, is a leading scientist who eventually takes on the Black Panther mantle herself. His estranged adopted brother, Hunter (the White Wolf), is fueled by jealousy. The White Wolf heads the Wakandan secret police and undermines T'Challa's rule.

Wakanda is a nation in a constant tango with both its isolationist past and its democratic future—a nation that thinks it's a little better than the rest. T'Challa is a model

LEFT: Darryl McDaniels of Run-DMC performs in San Francisco, California, in 2016. RIGHT: Kendrick Lamar performs at the Roskilde Festival in Denmark in 2015.

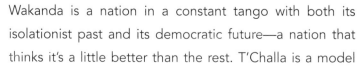

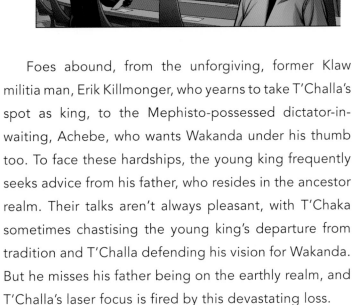

Foes abound, from the unforgiving, former Klaw militia man, Erik Killmonger, who yearns to take T'Challa's spot as king, to the Mephisto-possessed dictator-in-waiting, Achebe, who wants Wakanda under his thumb too. To face these hardships, the young king frequently seeks advice from his father, who resides in the ancestor realm. Their talks aren't always pleasant, with T'Chaka sometimes chastising the young king's departure from tradition and T'Challa defending his vision for Wakanda. But he misses his father being on the earthly realm, and T'Challa's laser focus is fired by this devastating loss.

Queen Ramonda, as seen in *Black Panther* #1, first published April 6, 2016.

T'Challa has had many loves over time: African American singer Monica Lynne, who was once his fiancée; the Dora Milaje warrior Nakia (who morphed into his nemesis, Malice); and most notably Ororo Munroe, aka Storm, the beloved weather witch mutant and best friend, who he married briefly. Yet the nation of Wakanda is his true love, for better or worse, and T'Challa finds himself hurdling the surreal to secure his nation's future and improve life not just on Earth, but throughout the universe.

T'Challa's excellence is the gift that keeps giving, as he's loaded with leadership responsibilities that take him to far-flung empires beyond the stratosphere. At various points in history, T'Challa was head of the Avengers (while still leading both Wakanda on Earth and its interstellar multiplanetary empire counterpart) and part of Marvel's Illuminati. He fended off takeovers of his nation by internal rivals like Killmonger and vengeance-seeking nemeses like Namor of Atlantis and arms dealer Ulysses Klaw, while simultaneously protecting Earth. He once foiled international espionage plots and fought off villains, all while running his country from a Harlem housing project. He led a team of sleeper agents on Earth and beyond. When Wakanda ditched monarchical rule for democracy, T'Challa, as ceremonial king, was expected to help lead the nation's transformation.

T'Challa is quintessential team no sleep. The *Thinking Man* statue could've been crafted in his image. T'Challa is always in an ethical quagmire that forces him to grow beyond measure as he outthinks and outpaces opponents. The young king places the good of Wakandans, and often the world, before himself, risking life and love—and he does so with an enviable cool and calm that cloaks an ever-raging intensity.

Black Panther's story prompts reflection too. We are forever in a two-way dialogue with the comic's myth. Black Panther is who many of us dream to be in our heroic swagger. However, his story also has expectations of its readers. Readers are to uphold the expectation of justice, keep the euphoric sense of victory etched in their hearts, and keep Black Panther true to what heroism should look like. It's fascinating that those who've penned

Part 1 of the Panther's Rage story line, from *Jungle Action* #6, first published September 1, 1973. This was also the first appearance of Black Panther villain Killmonger, pictured here on the right.

Black Panther attacks Monica Lynne's captors in *Avengers* #73, published February 1, 1970.

Black Panther in recent years were longtime fans of the book. They injected their own twist on the legacy, wholeheartedly aware of an audience who looked to Wakanda as a probable paradise.

It is this energy exchange between how we shape Black Panther and how Black Panther shapes us that I'm most interested in. Some say that super hero stories are the myths of the modern age. I'd reason that the

Black Panther myth is bigger than its creators, an idea held by fans, writers, pencilers, and the awed alike—a myth that channels lore and liberation. This comic has had untold impact on a dialogue that stretches times and obliterates conventions. It's a mythos that takes on epic proportions. One woman interviewed for this book said that Wakanda is as real to her as the Biblical city of Canaan. Wakanda as both societal goal and inner sanctuary resounds.

THE AVATAR

"In all of my situations I try to figure out what the super hero would do and I try to get as close to that as I can."

—Katt Williams, comedian, in an interview with
Arsenio Hall at Netflix Is A Joke

Not every comic hero is a symbol against colonization. Not every comic hero's evolution so closely parallels modern social change. People are infinitely fascinated by the sheer possibility that Wakanda and the panther lore embody, because T'Challa is a powerful symbol. T'Challa's heroic feats, whether defeating the zealot Achebe or the vengeful Killmonger, are as intriguing as the composition of the Wakandan world. The legend of the Dora Milaje, the all-woman Wakandan army, is as important for its real-world inspirations as it is for how it speaks to girls today. Shuri's journey as Black Panther is as spellbinding as her brother's.

Themes in Black Panther only entrench the legend—themes that also have a storied thread in cultures around the world. The quilted patches of ancient lore and public sentiment within the Black Panther saga have unfolded into a prescient way of thinking about futures, reenvisioning pasts, and reevaluating the now.

"You should've listened closer, N'Jadaka, there is more to this life than eternal power."

—Bast (*The Intergalactic Empire of Wakanda*, Book 1)

From the start, Black Panther was part of a larger conversation about what power looks like, who can have it, and the responsibilities that come with it. T'Challa's evolved role challenges the imagination around how one fantasizes about power in an aspiring utopia.

Perhaps *Black Panther* readers expect more of their hero, just as T'Challa's adoring and critical Wakandan populace does of him. He is a symbol of dreams manifest, a proxy for leadership, a stream of many rivers with an ancient resonance that is a guiding light for the future. To know more about Wakandans is to know more about ourselves. What is their guiding philosophy? What do Black Panther's victories say about our own potential?

Omolola: "T'Challa … he doesn't even have his Black Panther uniform. He's just T'Challa."

Shuri: "With or without it … T'Challa's never been 'just' anything."

—*Black Panther: The Long Shadow*, Book 5

Film critic Sergio Mims once said that no one Black story can address all the wrongs in society, balance the centuries of offensive images of people of color in literary history, redirect the impact of such portrayals, or teach undertaught histories. Perhaps not. That is a big ask. Such expectations are unfair to ask of any storyteller. Yet the creators of the *Black Panther* comic tried to do just that, and ultimately helped redirect the course of popular super hero narratives.

With all of their symbolism, *Black Panther* comics are both a deep and a really fun read. We want Black Panther

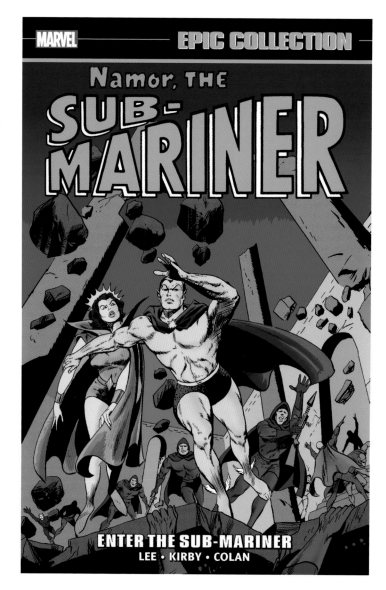

to win. A victory for Black Panther is a victory for the historically resilient. It is a victory for those who want to do what's ethically sound or need a determination refresh. Black Panther's is a story of fans who held the mantel when few knew his name, a story of readers remade by an icon, and an icon remade by them.

Namor, a sometime Black Panther nemesis, pictured on the cover of *Namor, The Sub-Mariner Epic Collection: Enter The Sub-Mariner*, published April 14, 2021.

ENCOUNTERS WITH THE FIRST KING

CHAPTER 1

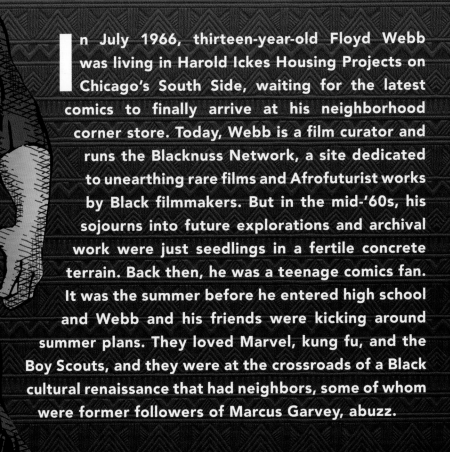

In July 1966, thirteen-year-old Floyd Webb was living in Harold Ickes Housing Projects on Chicago's South Side, waiting for the latest comics to finally arrive at his neighborhood corner store. Today, Webb is a film curator and runs the Blacknuss Network, a site dedicated to unearthing rare films and Afrofuturist works by Black filmmakers. But in the mid-'60s, his sojourns into future explorations and archival work were just seedlings in a fertile concrete terrain. Back then, he was a teenage comics fan. It was the summer before he entered high school and Webb and his friends were kicking around summer plans. They loved Marvel, kung fu, and the Boy Scouts, and they were at the crossroads of a Black cultural renaissance that had neighbors, some of whom were former followers of Marcus Garvey, abuzz.

The second wave of twentieth-century Black identity movements (the first being the Harlem Renaissance) was in full swing. Martin Luther King Jr. had led protests against housing discrimination in the city a year earlier, stoking youth movements as a new era of civil rights emerged. Webb and his friends grew up hearing the space poetry of Sun Ra, as the jazz icon recited in their neighborhood Washington Park. The teens were members of the NAACP youth program, along with a rising youth leader named Fred Hampton. One in their

fandom crew lived in a West Side neighborhood where comics were delivered before they reached the South Side. He relished calling his friends to "give the story away." This particular day, an argument ensued.

"He said this *Black Panther* book was coming," said Webb. Webb didn't know what his pal was talking about. "We said, no, that's an organization." Just a year before,

Martin Luther King Jr. addresses a crowd on a street in Lakeview, New York, on May 12, 1965.

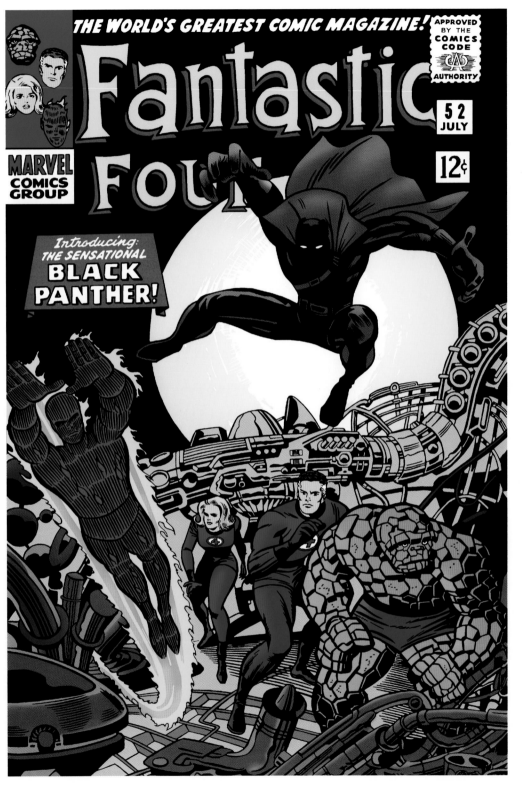

The first appearance of the Black Panther, in *Fantastic Four* #52, published July 1, 1966.

the Lowndes County Freedom Party, also known as the Black Panther Party, had been formed in Alabama by activist John Hulett and members of the Student Nonviolent Coordinating Committee (SNCC). Formed as a political party to run against the state's segregation, the organization registered Black voters and ran its own slate of candidates. They adopted a prowling panther symbol, at the behest of SNCC Field Secretary Ruth Howard—a symbol later borrowed by the Black Panther Party for Self-Defense in October.

Nevertheless, Webb and his excitable friend argued back and forth over the phone, with Webb reasoning that Black Panther was an organization, not a comic book character, as his friend insisted. When Webb finally got his hands on the now-historic issue #52 of *Fantastic Four*, T'Challa's debut did not disappoint. "We read it and it was so fun," Webb remembered. A mighty king of a hidden, technologically advanced African nation was just the comic hero they were looking for. "It's not only what we needed, it's what we expected."

It was a natural leap to see Black Panther as tied to a current hero, said Webb. Webb grew up reading J.A.

IS THIS THE PARTY YOU WANT?

WHITE SUPREMACY

FOR THE RIGHT

DEMOCRATIC PARTY

OF ALABAMA

or

IS THIS?

LOWNDES COUNTY FREEDOM ORGANIZATION

ONE MAN -- ONE VOTE

Rogers' *Your History* comic strips on Black icons and was accustomed to drawing real-world parallels to characters in comic form. "We had these strong feelings about who Black Panther was," said Webb. One in the crew was convinced that Black Panther was a reimagining of Patrice Lumumba, the Democratic Republic of the Congo's first prime minister after liberation from Belgian control. Even boxing champion Muhammad Ali, who often visited the neighborhood, came to mind. "We lived among Black heroes," said Webb, recalling the bevy of war veterans, Garveyites, and activists in the neighborhood. But he hadn't expected to see one in mainstream comics.

It may be hard to conceive today, but even as recently as 1966, Black people were rarely depicted as full human beings in mainstream media, if they were depicted at all.

Subservience of Black characters to buoy the white, usually male heroes was the norm. "It was profoundly radical," said artist Arthur Jafa of Black Panther's agency in an online talk during Carnegie Hall's inaugural Afrofuturism Festival. "It was so far beyond [the times] to have a Black character who was the match of anyone around him."

LEFT: A Lowndes County Freedom Party flyer.
RIGHT: Patrice Lumumba in July 1960.

The Black Panther explains the land of Wakanda to Marvel's first family (and readers) in *Fantastic Four* #53, published August 1966.

The Black-consciousness awakening bridged American civil rights movements, while the relinquishing of colonial control on the African continent ran counter to the pop-culture depictions of Africa. Even in comics, Africa was dominated by the colonial imagery of Tarzan. Yet the prominence of the civil rights protests on the evening news, the rise of Black Studies in colleges, and the issues of human rights were slowly changing media, including comics.

Turtel Onli, an artist who would later found the first Black-themed comic book convention, the Black Age of Comics, was fifteen when Black Panther debuted. "I was part of the Black Cultural revolution so the idea of an African civilization being at that level [of Wakanda] made sense," said Onli. "In his first confrontation, [Black Panther] beat the Fantastic Four. And back then nobody beat the Fantastic Four."

The moment was stunning. "Fantastic Four had just beaten Galactus, right," said filmmaker and future Panther scribe, Reginald Hudlin, who read his older brother's comic as a kid. "So, the Fantastic Four collectively beat a guy who could eat planets, and then Black Panther beat them. So, when you think about the implications of how powerful that makes the Black Panther, it is especially incredible."

The year 1966 was pivotal in the evolution of Afrofuturism, as well. "Sam Delany started writing *Nova* in the summer of 1966," recalled graphic novelist Tim Fielder. "A month or two before, Marvel

started *Black Panther*. What happens in September? We get *Star Trek*." The iconic sci-fi show normalized a vision of a future world where racism was no more. The character Lieutenant Uhura, portrayed by the late, great Nichelle Nichols, would later inspire and recruit women into space industries, with astronauts from Dr. Mae Jemison to Dr. Sian Proctor heralding her as a guiding luminary. After Nichols' passing, outpourings of love and gratitude from fans filled social media. "It was unprecedented for a Black actress to hold such a prominent role on a major television show," said Nate File, former Black Voices in the Public Sphere Fellow for the *Boston Review*, on the publication's podcast. "And Lieutenant Uhura's presence meant so much to Black people watching, that when Nichols considered leaving the show during the first season, Dr. Martin Luther King Jr. met with her and urged

CLOCKWISE FROM TOP LEFT: Dr. Sian Proctor gives a fist pump after Inspiration4, the world's first all-civilian mission to space, safely returned to Earth on September 18, 2021; Nichelle Nichols as Lieutenant Uhura in *Star Trek*, circa 1968; Dr. Mae Jemison aboard the Space Shuttle *Endeavour* in September 1992.

her to reconsider." File also interviewed author Tananarive Due, who contributed to the collection *Black Panther: Tales of Wakanda*. Due revealed that she continues to have "a deep visceral reaction" to more recent iterations of Uhura, even half a century after the character's debut. While watching *Star Trek: Strange New Worlds*, where Uhura is played by Celia Rose Gooding, Due said, "every time I just saw her and they called her Uhura, there were tears in my eyes."

LEFT: Stan Lee in 1972. RIGHT: Jack Kirby.

Throughout Black Panther's existence, there were readers who were deeply affected by the work. In the early years, T'Challa's appearance was such a stark contrast to African coverage in media that he stood out. But not long after his introduction, the Panther's relationship with readers would be marked by absence and limited access in the following years. Many who were looking for a Black super hero story didn't know the Panther existed, and many who loved it had to go on a quest to keep up with it. Yet, the lore lived on. Captivated imaginations didn't forget, and the dream that the story centered on persisted, as did the ones who told the Panther's story.

A SHIFT IN TIME

In 1966, Marvel Comics was deemed by fans to be the edgier and more relevant of the comics publishers. Stan Lee and Jack Kirby didn't shy away from tackling fascism, civil rights, dysfunctional families, or social issues. "Red Skull was Nazism; Magneto and Professor X were Malcom X and Martin Luther King. It just seemed [the creation of Black Panther] was more of them going down that wormhole," said Onli. While discussing Black Panther's early popularity, Stan Lee says he took note of Marvel's diverse readership. "I suddenly discovered that I had a lot of Black readers," Lee told *The Comics Journal* in 1990. He and Kirby wanted to make the first Black super hero in an African world that "looks like you're in a scene from a science-fiction movie of the thirtieth century!" They crafted a character who would become iconic.

Much of Black Panther's backstory, from Wakanda's tech advancements to the Panther's sophistication, was aligned with the aspirations of the era's youth movements and their new insights into African histories. "It made me feel like the politics of what we were talking about fit within a realm of possibilities. It didn't feel like fantasy to me," said Onli. "There might not be a Wakanda, but the idea of Black power manifesting at a certain level was possible."

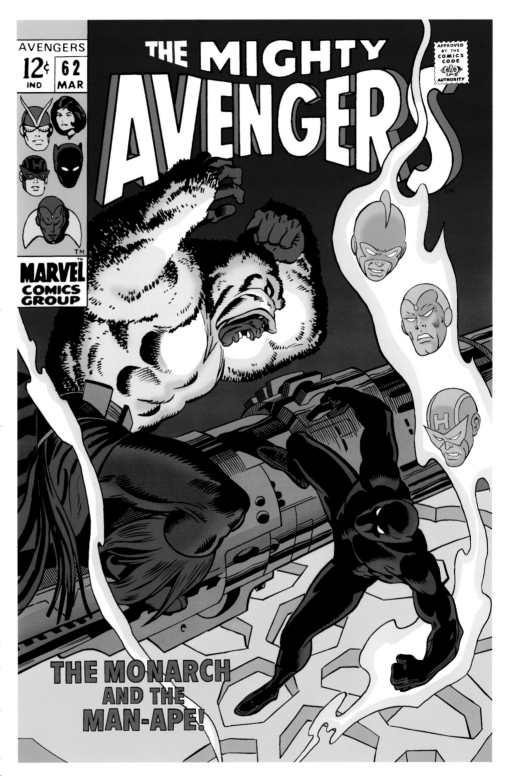

The first appearance of M'Baku/Man-Ape and the Jabari tribe, in *Avengers* #62, published March 1969.

T'Challa was featured in *Fantastic Four* #52 to #54, which marked Black Panther's arrival in the Marvel universe. Black Panther would go on to appear in *Tales of Suspense* #97 to #99, *Captain America* #100, and *Avengers* #52, before headlining the *Jungle Action* series (issues

Even using the term "Black" in Black Panther's name was a marker of the shift in identity. A person of African descent in the Americas calling themselves Black and openly connecting with African heritage in the '60s was a bold statement. "In '67, some civil rights leaders were still using the term Negro," recalls Onli. "Never mind calling oneself Black or African."

Comics writer Alex Simmons recalled a similar story for *Marvel.com* in 2021: "It was a time of protest for Civil Rights and equal rights and [against] the US involvement in the Vietnam War. In many ways the United States was facing its identity and clashing with itself on a grand scale. There I was in the middle of that trying to figure out who I was as a boy, and as a Black teen growing up with a mom and no dad. So the Black Panther character, this warrior king super hero, was a major discovery for me personally, not necessarily as a political figure standing up for all Black people or all Black males. I just saw him and enjoyed it and was fascinated by it and wanted more."

Floyd Webb even recalls stopping by the Black Panther offices in Chicago, founded in October of that year, and spotting the teen activists he saw there reading the comic. The book was a cultural phenomenon in the making—although only serious comic readers took notice.

"I always saw Black Panther as the African equivalent of Captain America," Hudlin told the *B&N Podcast* in 2018. "Captain America represents the best of the American spirit. He's moral. He's strong. He's fair. You know, he epitomizes all the beauty of the American experiment, and I felt like Black Panther is the same thing. He represents the morality, the spirituality, the legacy, the toughness, the brilliance of the African continent."

For the next few decades, with changes in the comics industry and the marketability of Black comics heroes in question, creators and fans would hold tight to their Wakandan memories, demanding more and ultimately getting the stories they deserved.

THE MIGHTY '70S

In 1971, Don McGregor was a Marvel Comics proofreader who took his complaints about the *Jungle Action* series to corporate brass. The series, all reprints of tales about the likes of Jann of the Jungle or Lorna the Jungle Queen, was riddled with stereotypes and followed white people and their misadventures in African locales. "I kept saying to them, 'I can't believe you guys are printing this racist material in the 1970s,'" McGregor said in an interview with *Vulture*. He was ultimately assigned to rewrite the series featuring Black Panther. The task was unique and McGregor dove into brainstorming, bringing his adoration of pulp-novel

Don McGregor.

The Black Panther announces to the Avengers
that he's taken a civilian job as a teacher and then
reflects on his time in America in *Avengers* #77,
published June 1970.

sensibilities to the work. Pencilers Rich Buckler, Billy Graham, and Gil Kane joined McGregor in creating an epic tale that *Vulture* described as "death, love, and revolution." McGregor titled the story in *Jungle Action* "Panther's Rage."

McGregor set the story in Wakanda and gave the book an all-Black and African cast. Since the Black Panther was typically fighting alongside other Marvel heroes far from home, McGregor was enthralled by the impact of the super hero's forays beyond the Wakandan borders on the nation's populace. Jealousy and infighting can surface when a leader is away, and latent problems can't go ignored. "I started working on the idea of a revolution within Wakanda because he's been away for so long," said McGregor.

He created the indefatigable yet empathetic foe, Erik Killmonger, a Wakanda-born rebel hell-bent on T'Challa's demise. Billy Graham, who also penciled *Luke Cage, Hero for Hire*, was among Marvel's first Black artists.

The plot twist would hinge on Black Panther's absence and the resulting turmoil brewing in Wakanda as he fought

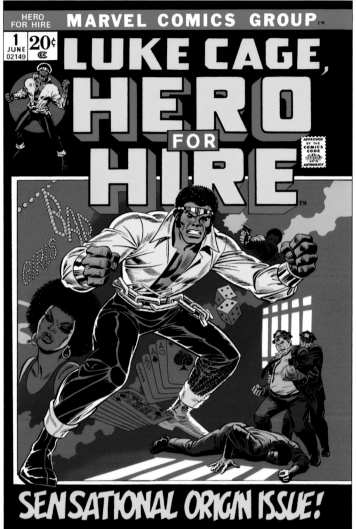

alongside Marvel super heroes. The high drama opens with T'Challa returning home with his new love, African American singer Monica Lynne. However, his home is in turmoil. He's challenged by Killmonger and is swiftly defeated.

"Wakanda became a *toy* to you—a bright shining *gem*—and on the day that *happened*, you lost your *kingdom!*" Killmonger says before tossing T'Challa over a waterfall, a scene later reenacted in a heart-dropping scene in the *Black Panther* film. The chaos that ensued in T'Challa's home country whenever he left to attend to hero work would become central to the character's story arc for decades to come.

In 1976, McGregor continued to bring his beloved character—and social commentary—to the page with "The Panther vs. The Klan," in *Jungle Action* #19. The gripping imagery by Graham was emotional and cinematic, as the African king took down the notorious real-world segregationist group.

Tony Cade, then twelve years old, remembers finding the comic in Paper Chase comics, located in Decatur, a

LEFT: Part 3 of the Panther's Rage story line, from *Jungle Action* #8, first published January 1974.
RIGHT: *Hero for Hire* #1, the first appearance of Luke Cage, published June 1972.

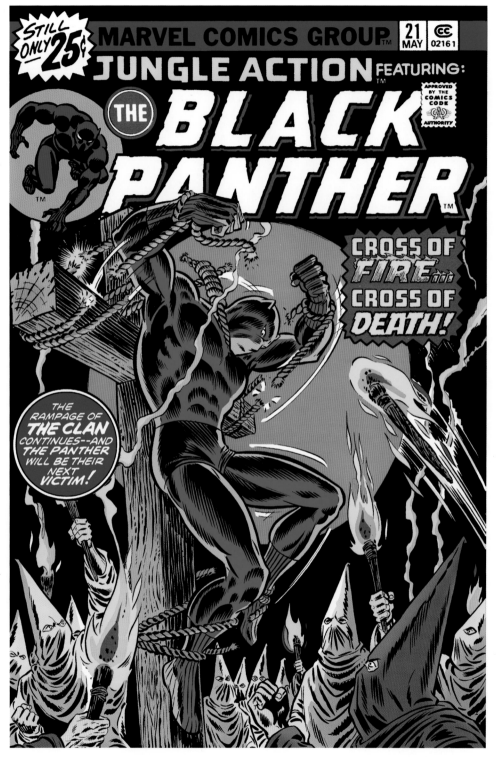

Part 16 of the Panther's Rage story line, in which the Black Panther takes on the Ku Klux Klan, as seen in *Jungle Action* #21, published May 1976.

suburb of Atlanta, Georgia. "During that time period in the 1970s as a young Black kid growing up in the south, the KKK was very real to me," Cade told *Eldredgeatl.com*. "The KKK was something to be feared. They were hosting cross burnings on top of Stone Mountain. It was real and it was terrifying. So when you had a character like Black Panther taking it to them, you were like, 'Hell yeah!' Even a comic book character doing what needs to be done helped to calm some of your rage. It allowed you to function in the world without being worried all the time."

One issue in the five-issue series opens with the terrifying image of Black Panther in flames on a cross, surrounded by white supremacists. "He is not a symbolic Christ!" writes McGregor in the issue. "Forget about turning his flesh and blood into some esoteric allusion to the persecution of contemporary man. This is the Black Panther, King of Wakanda. And he's made of flesh and blood. And the flames which consume the cross and his body prove his humanity. And the death-watchers, dressed in white robes, revel at his torment. And desire his death!" When the Panther breaks free, the heroics took on a deeper meaning.

The endeavor was risky. "Back then, comics were a much more mainstream form of entertainment so this

In 1977, Black Panther received his own self-titled book, written and drawn by the legendary Jack Kirby himself.

was a very gutsy story to publish," Tom Heintjes, editor and publisher of Atlanta-based journal *Hogan's Alley*, told *Eldredgeatl.com*. "This was the end of the *Jungle Action* title and they went out on a high note. They threw everything they had into that Klan story."

Jack Kirby took the reins of the *Black Panther* comic in 1977. Minimizing the internal conflict in Wakanda, Kirby played up the Panther's wanderlust side. T'Challa routinely goes on adventures beyond Wakanda's borders, searching for artifacts and uncovering lost civilizations. Representation aside, it was definitively apolitical. T'Challa traversed the world, befriending and battling King Solomon's Frog, Princess Zanda, the Collectors, and the Six-Million Year Man. The story weaves through the land of myths, including *Ali Baba and the Forty Thieves*, a Syrian folktale, and King Solomon's rumored tomb of treasures, including a frog with Mesoamerican designs. The campier style was described by one fan as "one of [Kirby's] goofiest and most entertaining runs." "That comic broke away from the grittiness of '70s cinema," said graphic novelist Fielder. "He kept it light and fun."

Black Panther's perfection held him high among the super hero world's idealists. The run was an example of a Black super hero character operating outside the world of social implications. But still, the book's very existence gratified fans seeking Black characters. T'Challa was nobler than Harlem's Luke Cage, the "hero for hire," whose book had debuted five years earlier. Luke Cage was a muscle-heavy guy from the neighborhood who used his heroics as a quick-money hustle. Cage, the bulletproof super hero who traversed Harlem streets, only took on assignments when he was paid to do so, a departure from super hero ethics that suffered from stereotypes about urban life. The nature of T'Challa's responsibilities—a king of an uncolonized nation wrestling with traditions and power—made the Black Panther inherently complex.

THE PANTHER DISCOVERY

The breaks in between *Black Panther* issues meant new fans would continue to rediscover the character for years to come. Many young audiences found the comic in an older relative's stash. Any *Black Panther* comics up to this time were hard to find and instant collectibles. Books were "inherited"—*Black Panther* comics and issues featuring his appearances were being handed down to the next generation.

"I remember it was the late '70s when I found the comic in my Uncle Phil's room," said Lee Owens IV, then an aspiring pilot in Chicago. "I thought Stan Lee made a comic about a super hero in the Black Panther Party. I just remember seeing that one and he only had one."

In the early '80s, seven-year-old Christopher Chaney was reading his uncle's *Black Panther* comics in Harlem. "My uncle went away to the military," said Chaney. "I found his comics at my grandmother's house." His first read was *Black Panther vs. The Klan*. "To me, Black Panther was this African king fighting to help African Americans. He fought the Klan. He was the ultimate. He was here in America to help us." Much of Chaney's work is with Black-owned media and venues. Uncovering Black Panther as a child helped shape his cultural consciousness.

Terry Gant, owner of Third Coast Comics in Chicago, was six years old and visiting his grandmother's house when he had his first Black Panther comic sighting. "The first time I learned about the Black Panther character was in the summer of 1977. My uncle Troy had a bunch of Marvel comics under his bed," he said. "Before that I didn't know Black Panther was a super hero." But he devoted himself to learning more.

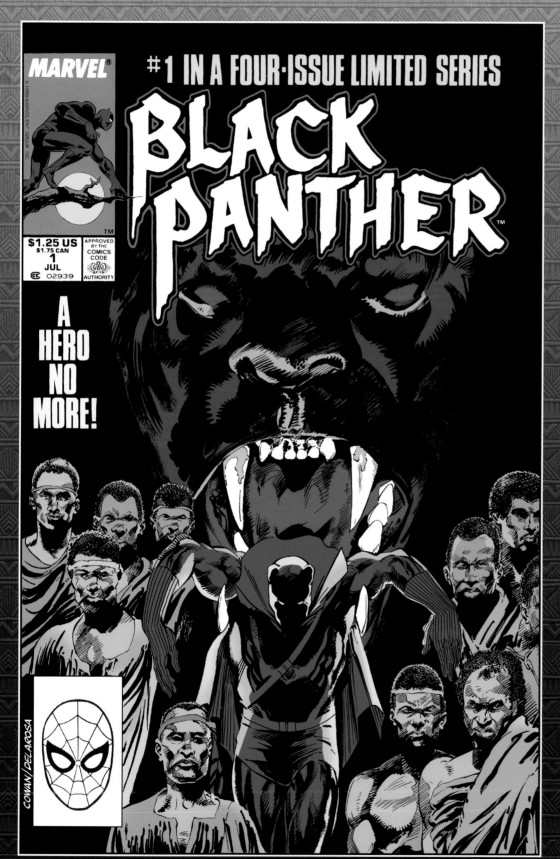

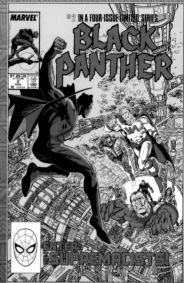

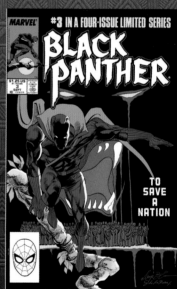

In the '80s, Black Panther appeared in *Iron Man Annual* #5, a follow-up to "Panther's Rage," by Peter Gillis and Jerry Bingham. In 1988, Gillis' *Black Panther* #1–4, a limited series, was issued. He also appeared in *Marvel Team-Up* #100 and in McGregor's *Panther's Quest* in 1988.

T'Challa mourns the loss of his mother, Queen Ramonda, in *Marvel Comics Presents* #14, published March 1989.

THE RESONANCE

Black Panther's rare appearances in the 1980s still carried the weight of his '70s run. "Any time Black Panther showed up in a comic, there'd be some kind of reverence. It was a big deal. The other characters responded differently to him," said Gant. "Writers were treating him with some kind of reverence like something that happened before mattered." The Panther's importance couldn't be denied. "Black Panther is the most straightforward, see through your BS, dude. Whether it's Reed Richards or Captain America, it's like 'oh sh—t,' Black Panther is back. The King of Wakanda Is Back."

Black Panther's symbolism carried him in those years. "You couldn't forget Black Panther," said Joe Currie, writer and creator of *Punx of Rage*. "Even if his appearances were brief you wondered 'who is that guy?'" Currie first read about Black Panther in the *Avengers* issues in the '80s. He didn't realize T'Challa had his own book until much later, a common theme for fans who stumbled upon the character in those years.

Yet fans from earlier years held the Panther as a beacon. "Black Panther's power was the people," said DJ Skeme Richards. Richards read the comic through the late '70s

and followed it through the '80s. A deejay who specializes in spinning rare 45s around the world, he holds a special place for *Black Panther* comics issued during those years and the cultural impact. "Black Panther said we have value in the white world."

The global anti-apartheid movement, designed to challenge the leadership in South Africa, reached new heights in the 1980s. Black Panther's battles in Azania, a fictitious neighboring African nation, were a metaphor for South Africa's real-life struggles. When McGregor returned to pen *Panther's Quest* in 1988, T'Challa headed to Azania on a secret mission to locate his stepmother, Queen

Ramonda. T'Challa and his heartbroken father had been under the impression that the queen had left her family for another man, but new rumors revealed that she was being held captive by Azania's leaders.

On T'Challa's journey, he came face to face with apartheid. "I had wanted to do a story with the Panther searching for his mother in South Africa," McGregor told editor Michael Higgins, as noted in *Marvel Masterworks: The Black Panther, Vol. 3*. McGregor realized that earlier issues didn't mention Ramonda at all, and he'd been nursing the South Africa

Nelson Mandela in 1990.

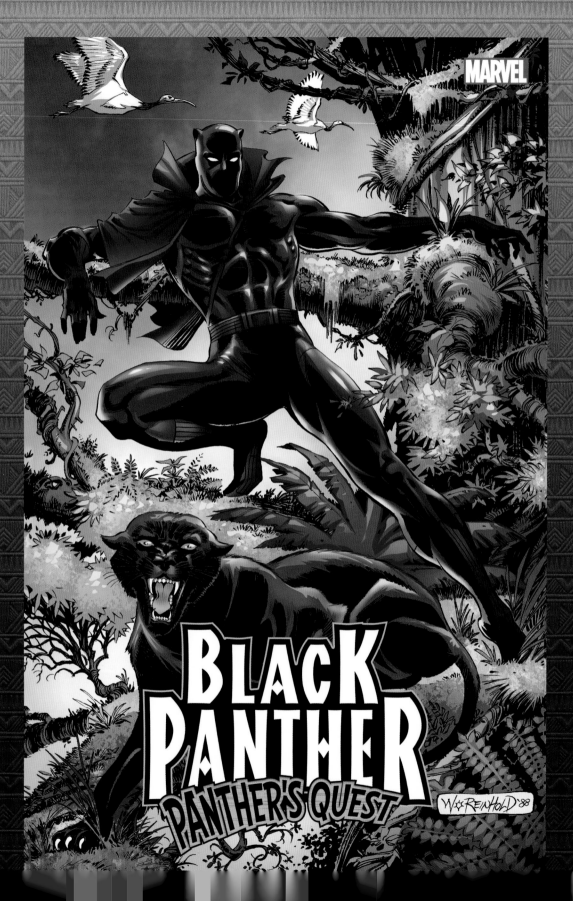

MARVEL

BLACK PANTHER
PANTHER'S QUEST

W. REINHOLD '88

After *Panther's Quest*, there would be no standalone Black Panther book for a decade.

setting for some time. When Higgins agreed to an apartheid story, McGregor initially thought the editor was kidding. But once he got the green light, McGregor's research included interviews and museum visits. "I began the first of many treks of my own to the Schomburg museum up in Harlem, one of the major places I did research on South Africa. The people working there asked me if this was really going to appear in a Marvel comic. I said, 'You got me. All I can assure you of right now is that I'm going to write it. If you see it in print, then, yes, Marvel did print it.'" The veteran writer was careful to craft a world where apartheid was alive and well—one where subjugation, segregation, violence, mob justice, and fear framed daily life.

The twenty-five-part series opens with a white informant who fears speaking to T'Challa in part because Blacks and whites can't be seen together in Azania. A racist militia, on the hunt for the informant, attempts to torture T'Challa before he breaks free. T'Challa takes refuge in a Black township and is rescued by Zanti Chikane, a miner who is sure to carry his passbook, an identification pass required for Blacks or Coloreds in apartheid-era South Africa. Chikane fears retribution from the police for aiding T'Challa, but eventually becomes his partner in the quest for Queen Ramonda.

Throughout T'Challa's pursuit, he is in the midst of the day-to-day violence of an apartheid regime. A white soldier firing tear gas from his vehicle nearly runs over a six-year-old Black boy named Theodore. T'Challa rescues the boy and the Panther fights the onslaught of soldiers that follows. T'Challa also rescues a spy, a Black man who likely reported T'Challa to the same soldiers. The spy was being subjected to a gruesome tactic called necklacing by a mob, a form of torture in which a tire is placed around a victim's body and they are set ablaze. Necklacing was common in South Africa at the time and McGregor used it as a device.

The same tactic is used to disarm T'Challa in government-stoked ethnic fighting. As T'Challa breaks free from the flames of the fiery tire, Theodore attempts to aid him and is badly burned. T'Challa races with the child in his arms to the distant whites-only hospital, where the child dies. A white physician affirms that he can't promise he'd attempt to save another Black life without the protection of someone like Black Panther. T'Challa is guilt-ridden over the boy's death.

The Panther evades a military manhunt, steals an aircraft, and eventually finds his mother chained to a bed in the home of politician Anton Pretorius. Ramonda reveals that while visiting her family in Azania many years ago, she was arrested at a protest against apartheid, locked in a detention center, and then sent to the home of the obsessive Pretoria, who held Ramonda as his personal prisoner. Ramonda is a reminder of those who "disappeared" after protesting government policies in South Africa.

McGregor's series was part of a global stance against apartheid. The comic was written as the anti-apartheid movement was stoking economic boycotts. In 1986, the United States enacted the Comprehensive Anti-Apartheid Act and corporations were pulling their business out of South Africa. Artists were creating anti-apartheid campaigns and songs to create awareness. But it was unheard of for a comic book to broach the issue. *Black Panther* helped create awareness among comic fans. Within seven years, apartheid would come to an end and freedom fighter Nelson Mandela would become the nation's first democratically elected president.

A MEMORY REVISITED

In comics, every new generation is introduced to a new iteration of their favorite comic character. The Panther wouldn't helm a book for some ten years.

With the shifts in how people could access comics switching from accessible neighborhood grocery stores and drug stores in the '70s to niche comic shops by the 2000s, Black Panther fans had to forge a new level of dedication. During most of the '80s and '90s, readers had limited access to the Panther, often discovering the comic through video game references, an older relative's vintage comics, T'Challa's moments in other issues, or oral history. Many didn't know the character existed at all. Panther fans of the '60s and '70s had outgrown conventional comic-reading age by the '80s, when the fandom was viewed as a teen pastime.

Gant critiques those comic lovers who abandoned the medium in the '80s, though Fielder counters that adult comic lovers of the '80s and '90s were ridiculed. And besides, "By the time the '90s hit, no one cared about Black Panther," said Richards.

BLADE'S RISE

By the turn of the century, another Marvel character would come to eclipse Black Panther in popularity. Blade, the roving vampire in the urban underworld, was another Black hero in Marvel's canon, now buoyed by a blockbuster trilogy of films. In fact, 1998's Blade was Marvel's first super hero film.

"Black Panther was the counterpoint to Blade," said Gant. "When people came out pumped about Blade after the movies, the old folks said, well, you don't know about Black Panther. People were dropping Black Panther on the Blade fans because they didn't know who he was. Kids who were goth kids in the '90s, they wouldn't have known what happened twenty years before in comics."

BLACK TO THE FUTURE

Characters like Black Panther and the heroine Torchy Brown, who was created by Jackie Ormes for Black newspapers in the '50s, and the psychedelic comics of Pedro Bell

on Parliament/Funkadelic album covers shaped culture despite their relatively limited reach in the mainstream. In 1994, Mark Dery's essay, "Black to the Future," explored Black perspectives in science fiction, referencing literature, music, and comics. The essay is most known for coining the phrase "Afrofuturism." By the end of the century, futurist-minded creatives and students would develop theories on Alondra Nelson's site of the same name. The "Black to the Future" essay asked why there weren't more Black creators in science fiction. Dery reasoned that African American life was inherently sci-fi. "The sublegitimate status of science fiction as a pulp genre in Western literature mirrors the subaltern position in which Blacks have been relegated throughout American history," wrote Dery.

It was the early days of the internet, but Black characters and comics by Black creatives were seminal in these discussions of new futures. Milestone Media's Black comic, Hardware; the Haitian art and graffiti influence on Jean Michel-Basquiat; and the Ikonoklast Panzerism lettering styles of Ramalzee were referenced too. A visual language was forming. Afrofuturism introduced a context in which to examine these art forms on futures and African or African Diasporic cultures. Onli once called this context rhythmism. The comics industry was wrestling with turn-of-the-century expectations. People were questioning comics' norms and expecting diverse representation. Some of the guideposts for how to move forward could be rooted in the Black Panther mythos.

There was another change. The sci-fi cyberpunk aesthetics and increasingly dystopian life takes of the 1990s ran counter to the optimism embedded in mainstream comics. Even the aspirations inspired by the super hero, which were typically a World War II-era nod to heroism, with clear heroes and villains, was no longer contemporary. Audiences wanted more complex characters with layered resolutions to society's problems.

In 1994, Mark Dery coined the term "Afrofuturism" to describe Black perspectives in science fiction. The term was later popularized by Dr. Alondra Nelson, who named her early Listserv Afrofuturism. *Afrofuturism* would evolve into an umbrella term aligning liberation, mysticism, technology, imagination, and Black cultures, and would give audiences a new way to frame works like *Black Panther*. The rise in popularity for Afrofuturism parallels a rise in the number of independent comics by Black creators, a change sparked by Turtel Onli. Onli founded Black Age of Comics, the first Black-themed comic book convention, which was first held in Chicago in 1998.

BLACK PANTHER

PRIEST • TEXEIRA • EVANS

MARVEL KNIGHTS

In 1998, Christopher Priest's long-running *Black Panther* series, published under the Marvel Knights banner, began. The Marvel Knights imprint attempted a fresh creative approach with more mature themes. Black Panther and Daredevil were launched under its banner. The critically acclaimed sixty-issue saga ran through 2005

THE PRIEST ERA

When Marvel asked Christopher Priest to write *Black Panther*, he wasn't sure he was interested. Ten years had passed since the Panther had his own book and Priest would be working from square one. But the opportunity to completely revise the character held some appeal for Priest. "If I could make him more substantial, a little mysterious, and bring him back to what Stan [Lee] originally envisioned for him, where he was a scientist and a physicist, that would interest me."

Priest would be the first Black writer to pen T'Challa's trek. He didn't want to be typecast as a writer who could only write Black characters. There were just too few Black comic characters to be pigeonholed, he reasoned. Fresh off the short-lived run of Milestone Comics, which he helped found, he had reservations about the support for Black comic characters. His resolution? He narrated the Panther's tale through the eyes of discombobulated white federal agent, Everett K. Ross.

John Jennings had just wrapped up his art studies at college in Illinois when he stumbled across Priest's issues in Star Comics in Jackson, Mississippi. The Megascope publishing founder and curatorial editor was captivated by the art. Jennings would later co-create the Schomburg Center's annual Black Comics Exhibition in Harlem, always remembering the visceral impact of comics. "Mark Texeira's cover caught me. The Black Panther was scaling the wall. I thought it was pretty dynamic."

Priest's zany take found Ross going through a bizarro world of comics lore as he attempted to document T'Challa's moves, a task he's always several steps behind

in comprehending. Priest used Ross' ironic humor to offset the Panther's regality. In this series, he crafted the

Christopher Priest.

origins of the Dora Milaje, centering on Nakia and Okoye as Panther's dangerous, alluring sidekicks. He created a nemesis, Hunter, aka White Wolf, Black Panther's white adopted brother, to lead Wakanda's secret police. Priest also fine-tuned Black Panther's mystique.

"Black Panther was a mash-up of Blaxploitation heroes of '70s action films and Nelson Mandela," said Jennings. Stanford Carpenter, Chairman of Black & Brown Comics Arts Festival, echoed a similar sentiment: "He's the man you want to be. He's not the guy next door." T'Challa's cool, calm dynamism aside, he was also a man whose royal duties prevented him from prioritizing anything other than Wakanda's future. He was always in the crosshairs of love triangles and unrequited love. Yet the Panther's no-nonsense attitude, might, and intelligence made him an instant hero for fans.

Gant remembers Black Panther's resurrection fondly. "So, in the '90s he has his own book. You have Everett Ross as the CIA dude. We hadn't seen Black Panther in

LEFT: Mark Texeira, photographed at the Paris Manga & Sci-Fi Show in 2016. RIGHT: Interiors from *Black Panther* #1, published November 1998.

a while. Next thing you know the whole story is about Mephisto, this devil guy. In three issues, Black Panther doesn't have to punch him or come up with some super science thing. He outwits him with his voice. He talked and charmed and intelligenced his way around a supernatural villain. He didn't have spells from Wakanda. He just came, circumvented the science of Western mythology, and beat him in one issue. I had never seen anything like this."

The style is surreal, with Ross' bosses and readers themselves often questioning Ross' take on the Panther's activities. The first issue opens with Ross sitting on the tank of a closed toilet, pants-less and clutching a gun. It's a flashback, as Ross in the present day tries to recount to his

former girlfriend (and boss) how he lost the Black Panther. The irreverent opening moment was evidence of a new grit and humor in *Black Panther* comics, and a fast-paced style comfortable with the playfulness of the uncanny:

> **The Story Thus Far:** Buster a rat so big you could put a Saddle on him, continuing to elude me. The Client and his personal entourage had, moments before, collectively leaped out of an open window, leaving me, Everett K. Ross, Emperor of Useless White Boys, to fend for himself among the indigenous tribes of

The Leslie N. Hill Housing Project. Zuri was into his third re-telling of how the great god T'Chaka ran the evil white devils from their ancient homeland. The bathroom had no door. I still had no pants.

Readers are essentially living in Ross' head, a mess of scattered recollections, casual bias, villain chase

LEFT: Interiors from *Black Panther* #3, published January 1999. RIGHT: Interiors from *Black Panther* #4, published February 1999.

turbulence, and insecurities. But the spy and the king have a mutual respect and trust—one that survives Ross' discovery that T'Challa dated his girlfriend (and current boss) in college.

Priest's Black Panther dealt head-on with the in-your-face sociopolitical issues that McGregor adored. He was also constantly thwarting international espionage, undermining crime in Harlem, fighting super villains, and moving between dimensions, with the help of Brother Voodoo in Wakanda. Priest built on McGregor's established tensions between the duties of super hero and king. Racing between his enclave in Harlem and Wakanda, T'Challa became a symbol of two worlds linked, Africa and urban America.

The rarity of the moment didn't go unnoticed for one Priest loyalist. "I had friends who custom bound every issue," said Currie. Black Panther's connection with audiences was affirming for Currie, who was just starting to create his own comics professionally. "That book meant a lot to people."

BLACK PANTHER SIGHTINGS, 1995–2005

Kevin Fair, President of I Am Games, a gaming event company, was an avid video game player as a kid. Fair first spotted T'Challa in the Marvel Ultimate Alliance video game in 2005. "If you were a '90s kid, the best way to see a character was through a cartoon or video game," said Fair. "I remember asking about Black Panther and someone describing him as Captain America but way smarter."

Brother Voodoo's first appearance in *Strange Tales* #169, published September 1973.

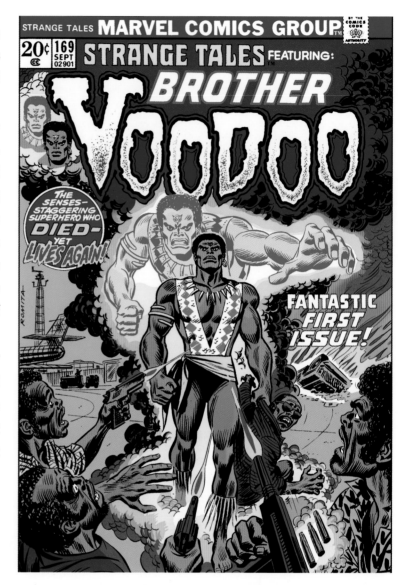

The Panther's occasional appearances in video games and cartoons stood out to comics fans. "I first saw Black Panther in a Fantastic Four cartoon," said Elgin Bokari T. Smith, founder of Pocket Con, a convention celebrating characters of color. Smith watched the *Fantastic Four: The Animated Series* episode with the Panther in 1994, when he was five or six years old. Regine Sawyer, president of Women in Comics NYC, saw Black Panther when she was collecting comic book cards at age eight or nine. "I remember my older brother talking about him," she said.

BLACK & WHITE: A CRIME NOVEL
PROLOGUE: TIN MEN IN THE GARDEN OF GOOD & EVIL
PRIEST & DAN FRAGA STORYTELLERS

LARY STUCKER INKER   PAUL TUTRONE LETTERING   JENNIFER SCHELLINGER COLORIST

MIKE RAICHT AND NOVA REN SUMA ASSISTANT EDITORS   MIKE MARTS EDITOR

JOE QUESADA EDITOR IN CHIEF   BILL JEMAS PRESIDENT

Marvel Knights' *Black Panther* launch captured the growing interest in grittier, more complex stories. However, the story wasn't well suited for kids. Children during the Priest run were discovering the character in other ways.

In 2005, film director Reginald Hudlin, then best known for directing the hip-hop coming-of-age film *House Party* and Eddie Murphy's *Boomerang*, joined Marvel. He wrote *Black Panther* #1–41 through 2010. During those years, Black Panther also appeared in *X-Men: Wild Kingdom* #175–176. He was included in Civil War and Secret Invasion tie-ins, too, and later appeared in *Fantastic Four* #544–550 and *X-Men: Worlds Apart* #1–4.

For many, these small moments with the character and his symbolism would carry them until they were introduced to Black Panther runs by Christopher Priest and Reginald Hudlin in the 2000s.

HUDLIN'S QUEST

It was Reginald Hudlin's childhood interest in Black Panther that landed him the opportunity of a lifetime. A chance meeting after his early film success led to Hudlin writing the next several years of issues. "Paul Power is a storyboard artist who introduced me to one of my heroes in the medium, Neal Adams," Hudlin told *Marvel.com*. "Neal was very generous with his time and felt I should meet with Marvel, so he set up a meeting with Joe Quesada and Axel Alonso. We talked for a while about comics, and at the end of the conversation [they] asked me what book I wanted to write. I was stunned, because that's not why I was there. But I left with the assignment of writing a six-issue *Black Panther* [limited series]."

Who is Black Panther? Reginald Hudlin sought to answer this question. Establishing the Black Panther for a new generation, Hudlin entrenched T'Challa in a broader historical arc, building on the Wakandan legacy. He also gave T'Challa a more conventional family life. For one, he added Shuri, Black Panther's tech-genius sister, who would later take on the Black Panther mantle herself. "I thought

LEFT: Reginald Hudlin attends a panel presented by the Academy of Television Arts & Sciences' Diversity Committee in 2008 in Burbank, California. RIGHT: Shuri's first appearance, as seen in *Black Panther* #2, published March 2005.

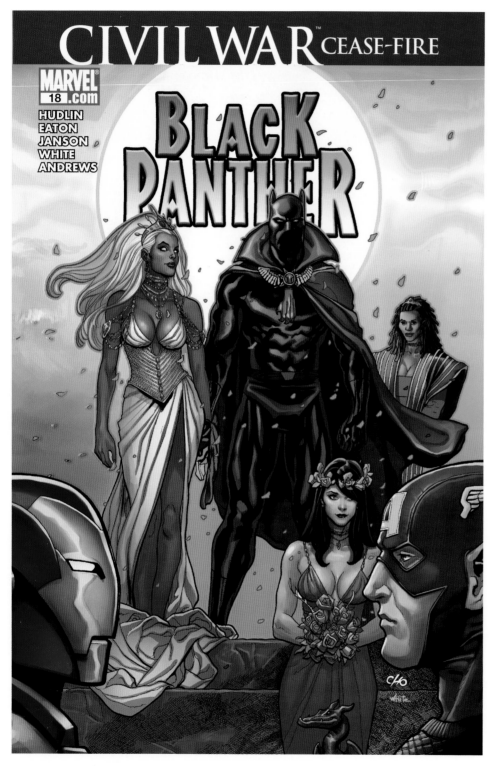

The wedding of Black Panther and Storm of the X-Men took place in *Black Panther* #18, published July 2006.

a girl would be great because I wanted everyone who read the book to be empowered," Hudlin told *Vulture*. He also expanded the lore of the Dora Milaje and situated the Black Panther in real-world history.

Hudlin's Black Panther spoke to Black comic-book-fan nostalgia. In Hudlin's run, Black Panther teams up with Blade, former detective-turned-private investigator Misty Knight, and Luke Cage to fight vampires after Hurricane Katrina in New Orleans, forming The Crew. "I wanted to write the stories I always wanted to see but never saw," Hudlin told *Vulture*. "What would Luke Cage and T'Challa say to each other?" Hudlin created a buddy-buddy relationship between the two, one that included dating advice in addition to shared battles.

He also introduced a romance—and an all-super hero wedding—between Storm of the X-Men and Black Panther. Luke Cage even attempted to throw a bachelor party in Brazil. The high-profile wedding in 2006 was covered in real-world media, like the *New York Times* and the *Houston Chronicle*. The posh wedding added a new glam factor to T'Challa, befitting a king. Storm's wedding dress was designed by costume designer Shawn Dudley, known for his work with the TV show *Guiding Light*.

"The marriage of Storm and the Black Panther was gigantic because it was the first time in comic book history

two Black heroes of any note were married," Hudlin told *World of Black Heroes* in an interview posted on *Hudlinentertainment.com*. "To say they are a power couple is an understatement."

Romance between the two African super heroes came as a surprise to X-Men fans, who were rooting for Storm to connect with Forge or Wolverine. But there were plenty of supporters too. "It was like watching Beyoncé and Jay-Z get married," said Terry Gant. "It was very Hollywood." Going "Hollywood" was exactly what Hudlin aimed for, hoping his framing would one day make it to the big screen.

Storm's brief marriage to Black Panther drew Sawyer into the story. Storm, the mystical weather witch of the X-Men, was Marvel's other reigning African character. She was also the resident comic-book hero for Black women looking for their image in the medium. "I knew about Black Panther through the lens of Storm," said Sawyer. She was intrigued by the refreshed backstory, in which the heroes' parents had shared history and T'Challa and Storm had met as children. In this telling, both T'Challa's father and Storm's dad befriended Malcom X when he visited the African continent.

Malcolm X in March 1964.

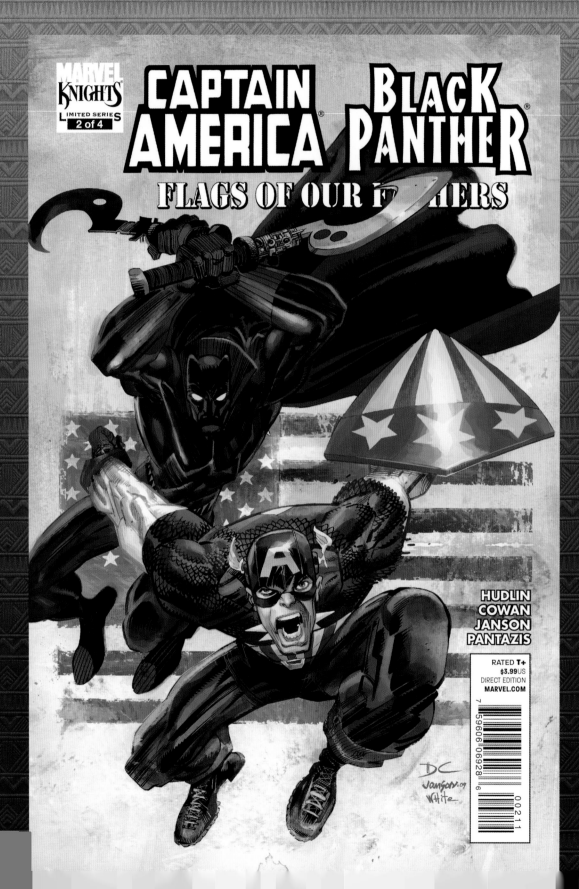

Hudlin and award-winning writer Jonathan Maberry wrote *Black Panther: Power* #7–11, which debuted in 2010. Part of the Dark Reign series, it includes the evolution of Shuri into Black Panther. He also wrote the flashback series *Captain America/Black Panther: Flags of Our Fathers* (pictured here), about Steve Rogers' first visit to Wakanda during World War II.

Hudlin reasoned that African royalty would be concerned about an heir and that a partner to the throne would be essential for the Wakandan kingdom. Even popular romance writer Eric Jerome Dickey would write a limited-edition love story between the two, inspired by Hudlin's take. "It was so dope," recalls Currie. Currie was both a comics fan and a reader of Dickey's steamy novels. "He made the relationship make sense," said Currie.

In 2008, Reginald Hudlin wrote *Black Panther: Black to the Future*, an homage to Dery's essay on Afrofuturism. The issue zips to the year 2057. Wakanda is a world leader and T'Challa is preparing the next Black Panther. For the first and only time, we learn that T'Challa and Storm's life together resulted in the birth of five children. Hudlin hoped his issue would answer the Black Panther issues he mulled over as a child. "I wrote the book to please myself, please people like me, many of whom were either fans who had drifted away from comics or people who may have never read a comic because they never saw a book like this," Hudlin told *MTV* in 2018.

BLACK PANTHER IN THE TWENTY-FIRST CENTURY

Hudlin situated Black Panther deeper in historical moments. In *Captain America/Black Panther: Flags of Our Fathers*, Steve Rogers bonds with T'Challa's grandfather, Azzuri, to fight Nazis in World War II. Gabriel Jones, the sole Black member of Sgt. Nick Fury's Howling Commandos, narrates the story.

Jones' story is a reminder of African American soldiers and Africans serving in World War II in segregated forces. It also evokes memories of African Americans who joined Ethiopian forces to ward off colonizers. Jones' heroism wins him an offer to become a Wakandan citizen. "Visual Afrofuturists don't have the luxury of creating comics that ignore history. We have to create on all sides of times to counter erasure," said Fielder.

Many of Black Panther's appearances in the early 2010s were priming the character for a new future. In 2011, the Black Panther animated series, created by Hudlin, debuted on BET. Hudlin was head of the television network and oversaw the project. "I wrote the comic book as a writer then green-lit the TV show as head of a network, then produced it as a producer. It's the only way that something that unusual would've happened," Hudlin told *Vulture* in 2018. The TV show was the first time Black Panther helmed a media property beyond the page.

"I watched the show with my daughter," said teaching artist and composer Sean Wallace. Wallace was an Avengers fan, but the cartoon was his first experience immersing himself in Black Panther's epic lore. "It was enjoyable to see this African mythology come to life. It was another way for me to share ideas about culture with my daughter."

Black Panther: The Man Without Fear, issues #513 to #523, ran from 2010 to 2012 and followed T'Challa living a new life as a schoolteacher in New York's Hell's Kitchen. Taking over Daredevil's spot and no longer empowered by the Heart-Shaped Herb, T'Challa relied purely on his wits and his own strength as he moonlighted to protect the neighborhood. David Liss wrote this book, along with *Black Panther: The Most Dangerous Man Alive* #523 to #529. The series elevated teachers in troubled schools as super heroes. It also provided insight into T'Challa as an everyman, whose greatness doesn't rely solely on herb-induced strengths or powers as a royal.

"It was this idea of a stripped-down Black Panther that didn't have access to all the tech," said Carpenter. "I

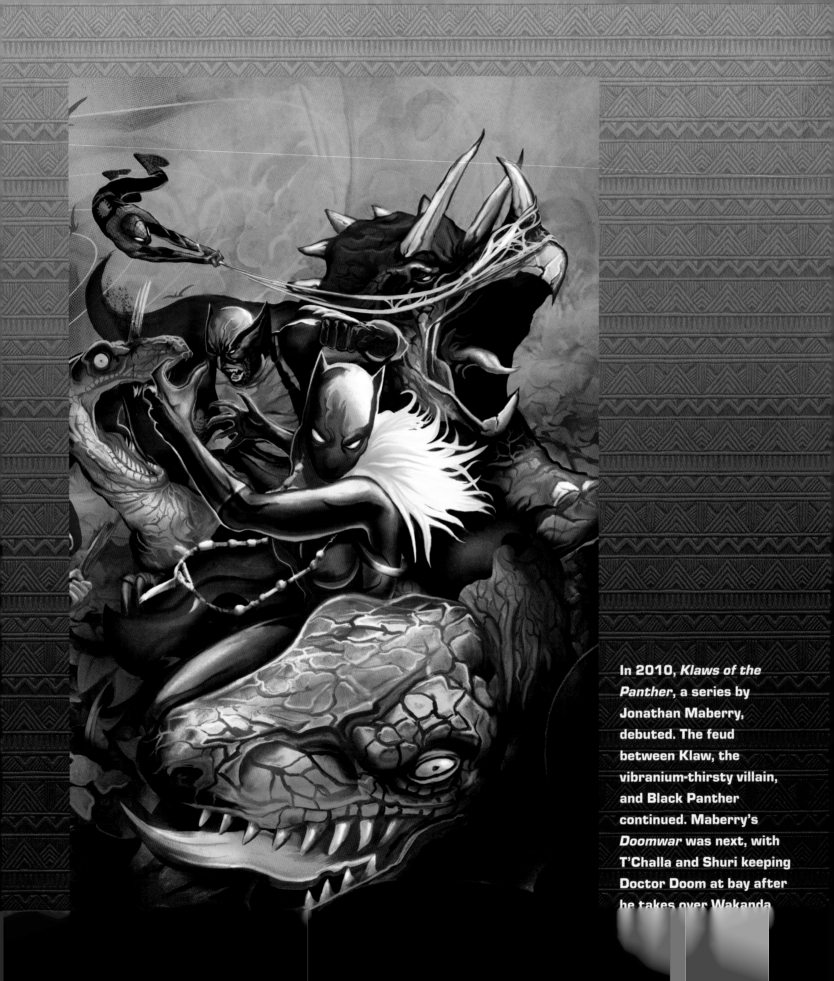

In 2010, *Klaws of the Panther*, a series by Jonathan Maberry, debuted. The feud between Klaw, the vibranium-thirsty villain, and Black Panther continued. Maberry's *Doomwar* was next, with T'Challa and Shuri keeping Doctor Doom at bay after he takes over Wakanda.

Black Panther appears in *Fantastic Four* #607 and #608, written by Jonathan Hickman. He appears in *New Avengers*, also written by Hickman, as the epic Secret Wars event unfolds. Pictured here: The cover of *Secret Wars* #1, published May 6, 2015.

Ta-Nehisi Coates at the Aspen Ideas Festival in June 2015.

thought it was interesting to see a street level, stripped-down Black Panther. However, I think Black Panther works best when he's struggling with his status."

In 2012, Black Panther joined the New Avengers. He also appeared in *Avengers vs. X-Men*, a series with cataclysmic fallout, and which saw T'Challa and Storm on opposite sides. In *AvX*, the Phoenix Force descended upon Earth and possessed the hell-raising Namor, and the Atlantean led his forces in a battle against Wakanda. The world was in chaos and T'Challa felt betrayed by Storm after she sided with the X-Men. In a shocking move in the fandom, the Panther annulled their marriage. Black Panther, the man fated to wed his nation, was affirmed.

THE COATES ERA

An award-winning social critic, Ta-Nehisi Coates' piercing internal reflections on the human condition were celebrated. Yet few knew he was also a Black Panther fan. When Coates was awarded the opportunity to write one of his favorite heroes, he used his same laser-sharp analysis to probe the Wakandan world as he had our own. Coates unearthed Wakanda's internal politics, and in his run, T'Challa must reexamine the throne itself in a nation that's inching toward democracy.

Wrote David Betancourt in the *Washington Post*, "In 'A Nation Under Our Feet,' the arc of the first 25 issues of Coates' 50-issue run, the Wakandan people are done with the hype after new villains forge

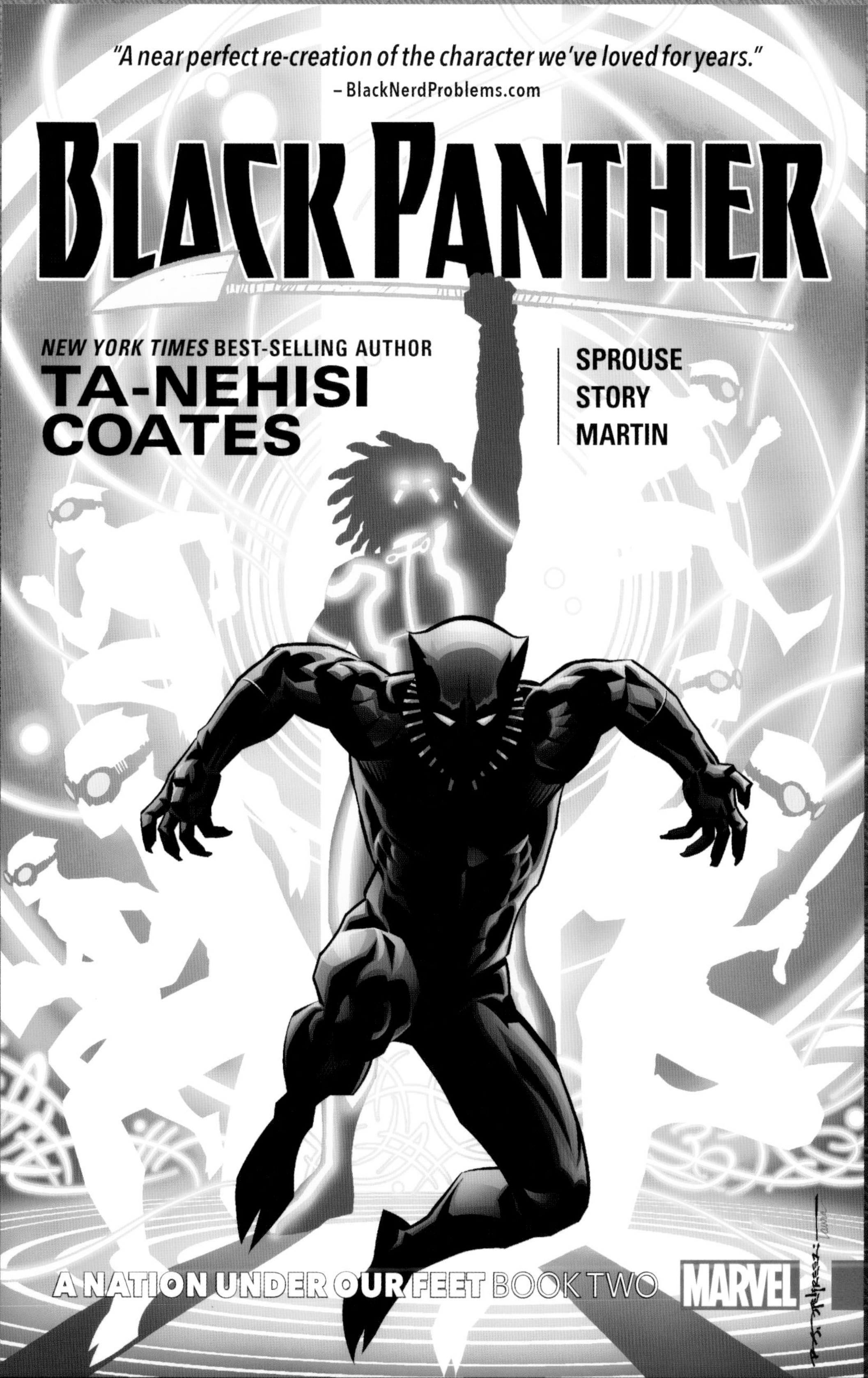

"A near perfect re-creation of the character we've loved for years."
– BlackNerdProblems.com

BLACK PANTHER

NEW YORK TIMES BEST-SELLING AUTHOR
TA-NEHISI COATES

SPROUSE
STORY
MARTIN

A NATION UNDER OUR FEET BOOK TWO

MARVEL

Ta-Nehisi Coates, best-selling author and essayist, wrote *Black Panther* from 2016 to 2021. The fifty-issue run, "A Nation Under Our Feet" and "The Intergalactic Empire of Wakanda," ran in tandem with Marvel Studios' *Black Panther*'s record-breaking success around the world. The film debuted in 2018 and changed the possibilities for creative works in Afrofuturism. With *Black Panther*, both the film and the comic, the cultural phenomenon in the making was realized. Pictured here: The trade paperback cover for *Black Panther: A Nation Under Our Feet* Book 2, collecting *Black Panther* #5–8, written by Ta-Nehisi Coates and published in 2016.

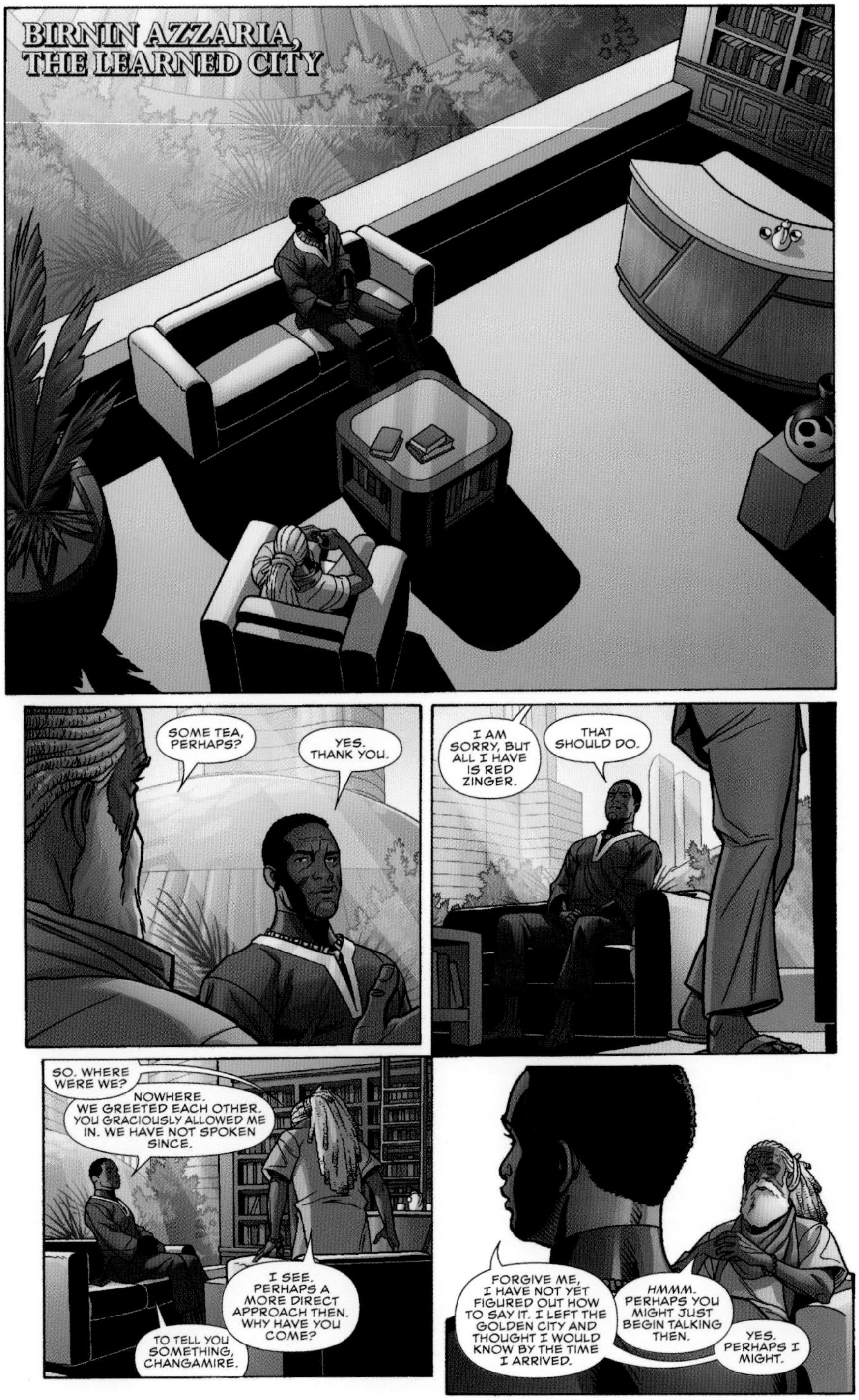
BIRNIN AZZARIA, THE LEARNED CITY
SOME TEA, PERHAPS?
YES. THANK YOU.
I AM SORRY, BUT ALL I HAVE IS RED ZINGER.
THAT SHOULD DO.
SO. WHERE WERE WE?
NOWHERE. WE GREETED EACH OTHER. YOU GRACIOUSLY ALLOWED ME IN. WE HAVE NOT SPOKEN SINCE.
I SEE. PERHAPS A MORE DIRECT APPROACH THEN. WHY HAVE YOU COME?
TO TELL YOU SOMETHING, CHANGAMIRE.
FORGIVE ME, I HAVE NOT YET FIGURED OUT HOW TO SAY IT. I LEFT THE GOLDEN CITY AND THOUGHT I WOULD KNOW BY THE TIME I ARRIVED.
HMMM. PERHAPS YOU MIGHT JUST BEGIN TALKING THEN.
YES. PERHAPS I MIGHT.

T'Challa consults with Changamire, Wakandan philosopher and personal mentor to Queen Ramonda, in *Black Panther* #16, published January 2017.

their emotions into an uprising. But not everyone needs to be hypnotized to see Wakanda in a non-glorious light. By portraying the Wakandan people as unsure whether they believe in what their royalty stands for anymore, Coates led the country to a parliamentary democracy. It wouldn't just be about what the Black Panther wanted; it would be what all of Wakanda thought was best for Wakanda."

While some readers felt a dissection of Wakanda's utopian status was unsettling, the evolution of the society into a democracy was intriguing. Who is a king in a nation with no monarchy? Plus, exceptional societies have class issues too. "I read this issue specifically because Coates wrote it," said fan Sean Wallace. Wallace, a teaching artist and history enthusiast, is always on the hunt for works with cultural content on Black and little-known histories. "It's not often that one of the great social critics of our time writes a comic. I was curious to see what he'd do with it."

In the tale, the Dora Milaje are splintering and no longer trust their king. A university professor inadvertently sparks a zealot duo willing to destroy all to take down the monarchy, and a king who's pulled in all directions must keep Wakanda afloat. In talking to a misguided rebel strapped to a bomb, T'Challa finds compassion. The man blames T'Challa for not saving his brother, to which T'Challa replies, "I am your king, boy. I am the aegis between you and all the great troubles that would break you on sight. That is my sacred duty. And whenever I fail, whenever Wakandans die, some part of me is lost."

When he commiserates with ancestors on the Plane of Wakandan Memory in *The Intergalactic Empire of Wakanda*, T'Challa reiterates his loyalty to the people. "Yes, I am a King, a nation incarnate," he tells Alkebulan, the Duke of Adowa. Alkebulan, a mighty leader who became a spirit to imbue his people with supernatural fervor in their fight against an invader, knows the victory and anguish in sacrifice. "Indeed, and there is weight to that, I know. As the Duke of Adowa, I bore it for my people. Then you know there is no singular 'me.' There never was. There never will be," said Alkebulan.

Much of this series is laced with historical references and symbolism. "I thought [Coates'] take was a really thoughtful run," said fan Jennings. "Alkebulan" is the African continent's original name, according to renowned Senegalese scholar Dr. Cheikh Anta Diop, who says it was used among the ancient Nubians, Numidians, and Ethiopians. "Adowa" is a reference to the first full-scale battle in the Italo-Ethiopian war, which was also the first Ethiopian victory and one that helped secure the country's high regard as Africa's only uncolonized nation.

Variant cover art by Jen Bartel for *World of Wakanda* #5, released in March 2017, depicting Dora Milaje warriors Ayo and Aneka.

The Intergalactic Empire of Wakanda also had several intimate spin-offs, conceptualized by Coates.

LEFT: Roxane Gay arrives for the 2019 Hammer Museum Gala in Los Angeles, California. RIGHT: Nnedi Okorafor attends the 2018 Emmy Awards in Los Angeles, California.

The Killmonger series, written by Bryan Edward Hill with pencils by Juan Ferreyra, detailed the popular foe's backstory. Shuri's evolution from tech genius into mystic shapeshifter in her brother's absence was written by author Nnedi Okorafor. *Black Panther: World of Wakanda* was written by comic writer Roxane Gay and poet Yona Harvey and illustrated by Alitha E. Martinez, with covers by Afua

Richardson, the first Black women illustrators to work on the series. Here, readers were introduced to Dora Milaje rebels, Ayo and Aneka. The couple's growing love affair and their distrust of Wakandan royalty puts their lives at risk. Gay and Harvey were the first Black women to helm a Marvel comic. A series that once struggled to get a solo series is now the source of multiple spin-offs penned by award-winning writers.

Coates continued the story with *The Intergalactic Empire of Wakanda*. The time-defying tale is a complete inversion of the Wakandan origin story. A nation that prided itself on fending off colonizers goes into deep space and takes on the role of that which they fought against. T'Challa sends a crew out to the far reaches of the universe only to discover that they have inadvertently created a mirror world of Wakanda with dubious values and slave labor. Everyone adorns the names of the heroes of their Earthbound Wakandan predecessors. One named for T'Challa's foe, N'Jadaka, runs the dangerous empire, which spans several galaxies. (N'Jadaka is the birth name of the villainous Erik Killmonger.) Here, T'Challa is a slave who must find himself to return home. Coates rekindled the love between Storm and T'Challa in this series, and also centered the tale in a remixing of African wisdom. The story turned Wakandan lore on its head, played with Diasporic themes of loss, flipped reverent gods into self-serving tricksters, and ran a race with memory recovery. By the end, T'Challa is a leader in two Wakandas, one Earthbound, one not. The tale's trippiness was reminiscent of Priest. "Coates completely turned our conventions inside out," said Jennings.

DIGGING IN THE CRATES

The popularity of Black Panther, forged by Coates' writings and the 2018 film's colossal reach, inspired many people to go back and read the beloved issues that they'd missed. Many new readers turned to works by McGregor, Lee, Priest, Hudlin, and more to understand the character's roots. A rising cadre of students of the comic medium also emerged at this time. With more

Afua Richardson at My Parents' Basement, a comic book bar, in Avondale Estates, Georgia, in 2018.

1

MARVEL

LEGENDS
BLACK PANTHER

ONYEBUCHI
FIADZIGBEY
ALLEYNE

RATED T
$3.99 US

001111

BONUS DIGITAL EDITION — DETAILS INSIDE!

7 59606 20166 2

In 2021, Marvel launched *Black Panther Legends*, a child-friendly story of T'Challa's upbringing with his adopted older brother, Hunter, the White Wolf. In the first issue, the two boys accompany their parents to an apartheid-era South Africa, where T'Challa also meets a young Storm. The series was written by Tochi Onyebuchi, author of the award-winning book *Riot Baby*, and illustrated by Setor Fiadzigbey. Also in 2021, Oscar-winning screenwriter John Ridley took on Black Panther with an arc called "The Long Shadow."

people looking to comics and science fiction for studies, a text as rich as *Black Panther* was primed for a new world of appreciation.

Graphic novelist Dameon Duffy read the Priest issues when they debuted. But the arrival of Marvel Studios' *Black Panther* film led him to read McGregor's work too. "It was really clear that he'd done a lot of research and that he respected all of his characters," said Duffy. A writer who has adapted Octavia Butler's

Kindred and *Parable of the Sower*, Duffy was interested in how white writers could responsibly write outside their culture and looked to McGregor's work. Duffy also liked the characters' monologues. "[McGregor] was able to invest himself in all the characters and not just the hero," said Duffy. "The reason Killmonger is such a cool villain is that you understand why he wants to overthrow T'Challa."

Others sought to understand the *Black Panther* comic's role in Black speculative writing. Clint Fluker, head of the Black Speculative Fiction Archive, is always looking at classic Black speculative works in a new or futuristic context. "When the movie was about to come out, I went back and read all the issues," said Fluker. What began as a passion as a student soon morphed into an academic interest. "I'm interested in how writers speculated on an imagined Africa and Black authors taking their stab at recreating myth in different ways."

JOHN RIDLEY'S BLACK PANTHER

After Black Panther's forays into deep space, he returned to a new Wakanda. Oscar-winning screenwriter John Ridley introduced readers to a Black Panther whose authority as king has diminished, as Wakanda embarks on its early years as a democracy. Written as a caper, the first volume of this new series finds Black Panther on a mission to find a Wakandan secret agent. John Ridley described his approach to Black Panther as a "very human, very grounded take on what it's like to be Black Panther. It's the story of regret in many ways."

John Ridley at a Q&A for his documentary film *Let It Fall* in October 2017.

Eve Ewing attends the Lena Horne Prize for Artists Creating Social Impact inaugural celebration in February 2020.

"Whatever you think about Black Panther, he is honorable and thinks like a king," said Carpenter. "In a nation that's a democracy, he ultimately struggles with being the last king. Even when you get rid of the monarchy, Wakanda is an exceptional nation. They haven't been colonized. They have this technology. They are the future."

T'Challa may no longer be king, but his sense of duty to Wakanda is deeply instilled. Working with the new prime minister, Folasade, and deferring to the council is not easy for T'Challa. His role may be in flux, but his commitment to Wakanda never wavers.

A NEW BEGINNING

In 2023, Eve Ewing became the first woman to helm the main *Black Panther* series. Ewing had previously penned *Iron Heart* and *Monica Rambeau: Photon*, and was also known for her nonfiction books on social justice. Chris Allen, an artist on the series *Stormbreakers*, joined the team as illustrator.

John Ridley's *Black Panther* story ended with T'Challa's surprising banishment from Wakanda, leaving Namor as the nation's protector. This is the point from which Ewing's story began. In an announcement of the book, Ewing described her run as "noir" and said that she found excitement in writing a legacy character. "I've always believed that the fun of writing these characters is not completely ignoring or undoing what your predecessor did, nor is it simply continuing with their story line—it's taking the reins from the place where they left the story, and accepting the challenge to make it your own," she told *Marvel.com*.

When Webb thinks back to the joy that he felt when he saw Black Panther's debut in 1966, he's glad that the character has an expanded reach. "I think everyone should have that experience—the experience of reading about a super hero in the African context," he said. "I spent a lot of time as a kid watching foreign films and reading comics. It was a good escape. I learned about things I didn't know." He still reads the Panther's latest sojourns. "I'll just quote Sun Ra," he says of explaining his fandom. "'There are other worlds.' Every time we go into these other stories, we learn. And it's good to go to another world, if only for an hour."

Wakandan Prime Minister Folasade, as seen in *Black Panther* #1, published November 2021.

THE PANTHER MYSTIQUE

CHAPTER 2

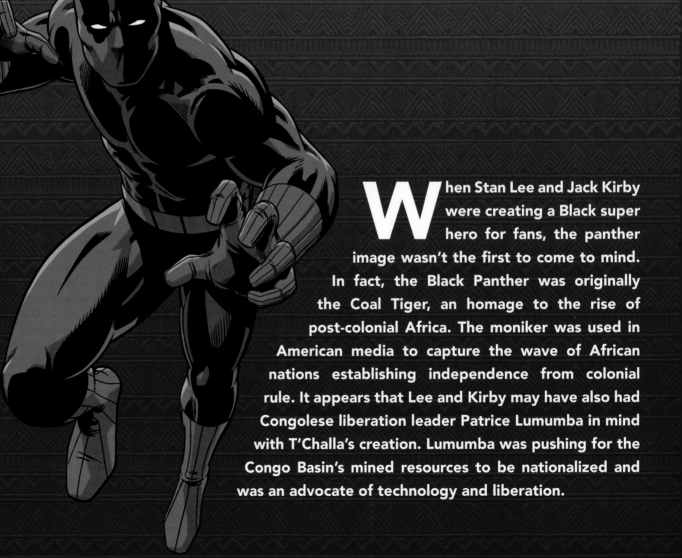

When Stan Lee and Jack Kirby were creating a Black super hero for fans, the panther image wasn't the first to come to mind. In fact, the Black Panther was originally the Coal Tiger, an homage to the rise of post-colonial Africa. The moniker was used in American media to capture the wave of African nations establishing independence from colonial rule. It appears that Lee and Kirby may have also had Congolese liberation leader Patrice Lumumba in mind with T'Challa's creation. Lumumba was pushing for the Congo Basin's mined resources to be nationalized and was an advocate of technology and liberation.

How the Coal Tiger became the Black Panther is a matter of speculation. But it apparently might have been an arbitrary choice. Stanford Carpenter researched the creation of black super heroes for a thesis in 2006 and in a conversation with Stan Lee learned that the birth of Black Panther and the world of Wakanda began as a plot device—a need for the Fantastic Four to stumble onto an unfamiliar advanced civilization. "The story could've taken place in South America or India. We could've had the first Latino super hero," said Carpenter.

However, in the months leading to the Black Panther's debut, the panther image was becoming a part of the American national consciousness.

"It's a spirit avatar," said curator Floyd Webb. "That's the avatar of Black liberation. We give it meaning by making it a part of our lives. It's not going away. It can be a panther with no writing on it and you know what it means."

Patrice Lumumba in the Congo in 1960.

A black leopard.

BIG CAT LORE

Black cats are either feared or revered, depending on who you ask. Whether they're a witch's aid or an ancient warrior's inspiration, black cats big and small are etched in collective storytelling consciousness. "It's an animal that's an intermediary between different realities," said Rita Lucarelli, Associate Professor of Egyptology at University of California, Berkeley. "The cat is a mystical animal of another dimension." The black panther appears to be a reversal of the lore of black cats as unlucky or the sign of bad omens, establishing a new nobility for black felines.

Mythology around the world typically associates leopards and jaguars with strength, spirituality, wisdom, and multidimensionality. "The leopard is a travel companion for people transitioning from one realm to the next," said Faye Edwards, owner of Faie Afrikan Art Gallery in Chicago. "In ancient times, a courageous monarch in some African cultures who ruled over other monarchs was called a leopard."

They have special significance in Indigenous American lore and spirituality. "In Aztec and Mayan culture, jaguars were one of the top two highest class of warrior," said artist Erick "ROHO" Garcia. Garcia often paints jaguars as protective symbols in his work. In Ho-Chunk and Potawatomi culture, water spirits sometimes appear as water panthers who alternately stir and calm the waters beyond sight. "Water spirits are neither bad nor good," said Rob Callahan, an Indigenous speculative fiction writer. The characterization of the waters as a panther reflects the awe, reverence, and terror that oceans and lakes can hold. "Water spirits are just off doing what water spirits do regardless of human activity."

PANTHER PRIDE

Black panthers are sights to behold—fast, strong, sleek, and with stunning beauty. "They're majestic. They're glorious," said Garcia. Power, agility, and wisdom—all traits that T'Challa is known for—constitute a panther's intrigue. They track their prey and are masters of camouflage. By the time you see one, it's upon you. They are vicious and foreboding. They are regal in bearing. Their nocturnal nature adds to their mystique.

Jaguar carving, Paseo Montejo in Merida, Mexico.

often situated, they are more commonly found in southwestern China, southern India, Burma, Malaysia, and Nepal. Black jaguars can be found in Mexico, Paraguay, Guatemala, Belize, Bolivia, and Brazil. Wherever they are, these felines are rare. And if you're in the vicinity of one, it will see you before you see it.

"No animal is more elusive," said Will Burrard-Lucas, a wildlife photographer who photographed the animal in the city of Laikipia in Kenya. It was the first panther spotted in the area in close to a century. "Nobody I knew had ever seen one in the wild and I never thought that I would either."

Panther agility is boundless. They can climb up trees and climb down them headfirst. They can jump ten feet in the air and can run as fast as thirty-six miles per hour. They're also powerful swimmers, have retractable claws, possess a powerful jaw, and can hear high frequencies.

An animal's symbolism is rooted in its prowess. "You can almost look at the animals in African art and tell the symbolism," said Edwards. "No one has to tell you a lion has strength, you can look at the body."

Black panthers are solitary hunters shrouded in an air of intensity. "There's this sense of focus," says teaching artist and composer Sean Wallace. "That's an interesting metaphor for meditation, to hold a thought in mind for as long as it takes to achieve whatever that is."

"Leopards have such great eyesight, they can see what others can't see," said Edwards. Moreover, panther balance is enviable. "No matter how they fall, they always land on their feet," said Wallace. "That sense of balance. There's a metaphor there for, regardless of what

Black panthers are also somewhat misunderstood. For one, they're not their own species, but are actually leopards or jaguars with dark pigmentation. "It's not really black, per se. If you get closer, you see that they still have these patches," said Garcia.

While there are black leopard sightings in Ethiopia and Kenya, countries near where the fictional Wakanda is

A black leopard perched on a tree branch.

happens in life, you land on your feet, ready to make the next move."

The black panther is the national symbol of Gabon, a nation of two million in central Africa, where it symbolizes strength and will.

As an aesthetic, panthers demonstrate power and grace. "It's strength, sleekness, mystique are attractive," said comic book illustrator N. Steven Harris. "Culturally, Black people value style, finesse, and the black panther captures that and beauty."

This feline essence is all over T'Challa, both when he dons the Panther nanotech suit and without it.

A scene from a protest against the incarceration of members of the Black Panthers in New York on November 17, 1969.

Afro-American solidarity with the oppressed People of the world

CULTURE MOVES THE MESSAGE FORWARD

The Black Panther Party spread its ideas and political messages through posters, music, newspapers, speeches, and photography. They used poetry to inspire the people. The Party's way of connecting art and politics is part of a rich creative tradition that continues today.

A SYMBOL UNFOLDS

When the Black Panther Party for Self-Defense formed in 1966, three months after the launch of the *Black Panther* comic, they looked to the Lowndes County Freedom Party in Alabama for inspiration. Born out of the SNCC lead voting rights movements in the South to counter Black voter suppression and violence against Black residents, the LCFP

A poster by Emory Douglas created for the Black Panther Party newspaper, seen in an exhibition in Oakland, California, in 2016.

was formed in 1965 to create a slate of Black candidates and register voters. At the time, literacy rates were low and Alabama state law required political parties to have a logo on their ballot. LCFP adopted the black panther as their mascot.

Early brochures were very frank about the animal's symbolism. "Their symbol is the black panther which stands for courage, determination, and freedom," one LCFP brochure, printed in October 1966, read. "It was chosen as an appropriate response to the racist Alabama Democratic symbol and its symbol the white rooster and its slogan White Supremacy for The Right."

Activist and SNCC member Stokely Carmichael is credited with coming up with the black panther symbol

idea. Essayist Lincoln Cushing writes in his article "The Women Behind the Black Panther Logo" in *DesignObserver.com* that several women in the organization shaped the panther's design.

"I was working in the Atlanta office of Student Nonviolent Coordinating Committee [SNCC] when I was approached by [SNCC field organizer] Stokely Carmichael because he knew I'd gone to the High School of Music and Art," said Dorothy "Dottie" Zellner, a SNCC field officer. "He'd gone to a sister school, Bronx High School of Science. He asked me to draw a panther for the Lowndes County Freedom Organization campaign. I said no, I wasn't that capable an artist." The article states that Zellner asked her husband at the time, Bob, to take a photo of a panther at the Atlanta Zoo for reference. Bob later recounted that SNCC member James Forman asked who in the office could draw. "Dottie drew it so it would reproduce well in black and white—a panther with curled tail, bared teeth, and pronounced whiskers, ears perked up."

LEFT: A plaque at the entrance to the headquarters of the Black Panther Party in Algeria. RIGHT: Stokely Carmichael in 1967.

The Prairie View A&M cheer squad and panther mascot.

"We chose for the emblem a black panther, a beautiful black animal which symbolizes the strength and dignity of Black people, an animal that never strikes back until he's back so far into the wall, he's got nothing to do but spring out," Carmichael told the Students for a Democratic Society (SDS)–sponsored "Black Power and Its Challenges" conference at U.C. Berkeley, lines quoted in Cushing's article. "Yeah. And when he springs he does not stop."

Zellner's second draft was based off a sketch by another SNCC member, Ruth Howard. Howard had based her rendition on HBCU (historically Black college or university) Clark College's (now Clark Atlanta University) mascot. (Prairie View A&M, an HBCU in East Texas, founded in 1876, also has a black panther mascot.) Carmichael gave Zellner Howard's sketch to work from. "I cleaned it up, added better whiskers, and made it black, at his request," said Zellner in *DesignObserver.com*.

Community activist Mark Comfort brought the panther name and logo to the San Francisco Bay Area after he formed the Black Panther Project of the Oakland

Direct Action Committee in 1965. By the time Lisa Lyons borrowed the LCFP image for Black Power Day posters and buttons, in conjunction with the Black Panther Party in the fall of 1966, she said the image was already a nationally recognized symbol for Black liberation.

This notion of an animal forced to defend itself as a metaphor was echoed by LCFO co-founder, John Hulett. "The black panther is a vicious animal, as you know," said Hulett, according to SNCC Digital Gateway. "He never bothers anything, but when you start pushing him, he moves backward, backward, and backward, and then he comes out and destroys everything that's in front of him."

The Black Panther held special resonance in the months leading up to the creation of the comic hero. However, it's possible that Lee and Kirby could've looked to another inspiration.

In World War II, the 761st Tank Battalion, one of three African American units in the then-segregated

Black Panther Party banners curated by Lisbet Tellefsen, an Oakland-based archivist, publisher, curator, and collector, hang inside Jilchristina Vest's Oakland, California, home, which houses a small museum dedicated to the Black Panthers.

W.76 WORLD WAR II FRENCH SOLDIERS FILL THE HANDS OF AMERICAN NEGRO SOLDIERS WITH   961-S

military, called themselves the Black Panthers. They wore a growling black panther on a patch affixed to their uniforms and had the motto "come out fighting." The unit would have to fight racism at home and face fierce combat in Europe. In fact, baseball legend Jackie Robinson was a part of the battalion and later

During World War II, French soldiers share candy with Black American soldiers in France in 1945.

reassigned, having never seen battle, because he refused to sit at the back of a segregated military bus in Fort Hood, Texas. Nevertheless, the Black Panthers fought with the Allied forces in the Battle of the Bulge and helped liberate Gunskirchen, a subcamp of the Mauthausen concentration camp. The unit was awarded four campaign ribbons, 11 Silver Stars, 69 Bronze Stars, and about 300 Purple Hearts. Their efforts would help lead to the end of military segregation in 1948.

LEOPARD MEN IN LITERATURE

Panthers and those who gain power from them had a storied if not problematic emergence in late nineteenth-century Western writing. The first reference to a black-panther-imbued hero in Western literature may have been a novel written in 1864. *The Black Panther: Or A Boy's Adventures Among the Redskins* by C.F. Lascelles Wraxall followed the journey of an African American boy who becomes a leading warrior amongst Native Americans. Wraxall, an Englishman, admittedly, had never been to the western United States.

Another popular depiction of the animal comes from Rudyard Kipling's *The Jungle Book*, in which Bagheera, a black panther and the animal pal of the lead character, Mowgli, is a protector, feared by others but caring for his human friend in the Indian jungles.

In other cases, the ferociousness of African leopards was used to stoke fear. The African stereotypes used in Tarzan books spawned from sensationalized fears of resistance in the Congo. In real life, the Anyoto Leopard Men, a secret society in the eastern Congo, were an anti-colonial force in the 1890s through 1935 that wielded power over the local people and used leopard, although not specifically *black* leopard, accoutrements. Leopard hides and teeth were sacred and part of many chiefs' regalia. The Anyoto Leopard Men left leopard paw prints near victims, a mix of colonizers, challengers, and those who betrayed them. "The Anyoto society also had a psychological effect on the colonial establishment which was unable to get a grip on the society despite its

The Jungle Book by Rudyard Kipling features a black panther named Bagheera.

A relief depicting the goddess Bast.

investigations and the strength with which it is fought," said researcher Vicky Van Bockhaven.

But this anticolonial posturing got lost in Western storytelling, riddled with fear and fascination. "The secrecy surrounding the society and its ritual approach, imitating attacks of a leopard, played very much on the imagination of colonizers and missionaries and engendered awe," she wrote. The mischaracterization would shape Western fiction about Africa for decades to come. Black Panther's reworking in comic books and other popular media helped counter the narrative.

BAST RULES

Egyptian goddess Bast was adopted as Wakanda's reigning deity. In Wakanda she appears as a giant looming panther spirit, a young child, or a sultry, adoring goddess. Originally depicted in Ancient Egypt with a lioness head and a human body, much like her sister, Sekhmet, Bast was later symbolized by cats or a woman with a cat's head. In magical text, Bast and Sekhmet, as lion and cat, are sometimes blurred. Bast was first worshipped in the third millennium BCE in Lower Egypt and her popularity continued throughout the first millennium in Greece.

"She's called goddess of the rising sun. The sacred one. The all-seeing eye," said Rita Lucarelli. "She's the most important cat goddess of all."

Bast, also known as Bastet, had many evolutions over the centuries, but her feline power and cat symbolism remained. She's also represented as a musician, often clutching the sistum, a percussion instrument used in rituals. Mummified cats were found in temples in her honor.

"You have to please the goddess," said Lucarelli. Bubastis was her resident city in Egypt, home to an assortment of decadent festivals to celebrate her wonder.

"Bast was a goddess of love but also feminine pleasure. At the same time, she could be aggressive," said Lucarelli. "There is a great feminine prowess, but at the same time she can get really destructive."

The goddess is sometimes described as the eye of Ra or the eye of Osiris when she's sent to destroy enemies, like when she slew Apep, the bringer of evil. However, her

LEFT: The Egyptian coffin of a cat. RIGHT: Bronze figurines of the goddess Bast, as a cat (left) and a cat-headed woman.

She is a protector of Ra, the sun, often shielding him from Apep, the symbol of chaos. Bast is sometimes called the eye of Ra and, since she doubles as a moon goddess, she is also known as the eye of the moon.

Although Bast is symbolized by a cat, this cat is not today's house cat. In fact, Bast in her Egyptian context feels more like a panther, says Lucarelli. Nor is Bast's name a substitute for *feline* in old languages. No one knows what Bast's name truly means, said Lucarelli.

Although Bast in the Egyptian world isn't a panther per se, there's increasing evidence that black panthers had a larger role in Egyptian society than popularly believed. A statue of King Tutankhamun, often called King Tut, standing upon a black panther was found in his sepulcher. The discovery forged a rethinking of Ancient Egyptian symbols. As Ancient Egypt is studied more in the context of African nations to the south, more relationships between Egypt's mythology and the mythos of leopards and black leopards in the region will be revealed, said Lucarelli.

Those who honor Bast today celebrate her cat-like traits of being feminine, playful, graceful, and protective. In the world of Wakanda, her feline dynamic and protector qualities imbue T'Challa's path, adding another dynamic to the panther's ferocious image. This presentation parallels the African American uses of the panther. "When I was in the breakfast program with the Panthers [the organization], we didn't see them as dangerous, but as protective," said Faye Edwards. The same goes for T'Challa. "T'Challa could be dangerous in terms of his skills and abilities but he was more of a protective figure to me," said Edwards. "The suit made him look fierce but he didn't have that ferociousness about him."

strongest attribute was that of protector. "Bastet when she's represented is always black," said Lucarelli. "Sometimes presented in green stone. Otherwise, you have a heavy stone, black stone figures."

Bast is both a moon and a sun goddess, sometimes seen in a solar boat traveling the sky with her father, Ra.

A gilded wooden statue of Tutankhamun riding a black varnished panther.

Those who honor Bast today also see her as a symbol of independence. "She's an independent spirit, but also intuitive," said Lettie Sullivan, head of The Goddess Ministry. Wakandans adore Bast. She is the source of all, their fiercest defender, and the wellspring of their prosperity.

However, her ways are questioned when she takes the form of a bratty child on a dystopian Wakandan planet in *The Intergalactic Empire of Wakanda*. The goddess takes on near trickster qualities, similar to the Yoruba god, Esu, in this form. When T'Challa topples his oppressors in the series, the child Bast overpowers her captives as well, and becomes a fierce goddess woman. "How can an entity be both mother and child?" she asks as she overpowers her victim. "How can the maker of galaxies, too, be made by them?" Just as T'Challa blames her for the tragedy, she reminds him that he created the scenario by sending Wakandans into space to begin with. Bast's evolving role in Wakanda as not just an exemplar of excellence but also one who takes on unusual ways to demand excellence of those she empowers is a new iteration. No longer simply the fiercely protective mother cat spirit, Bast may be moving closer to her Ancient Egyptian lore. Ancient Egyptian gods take on many transformations, says Lucarelli. The panther as avatar is always among us.

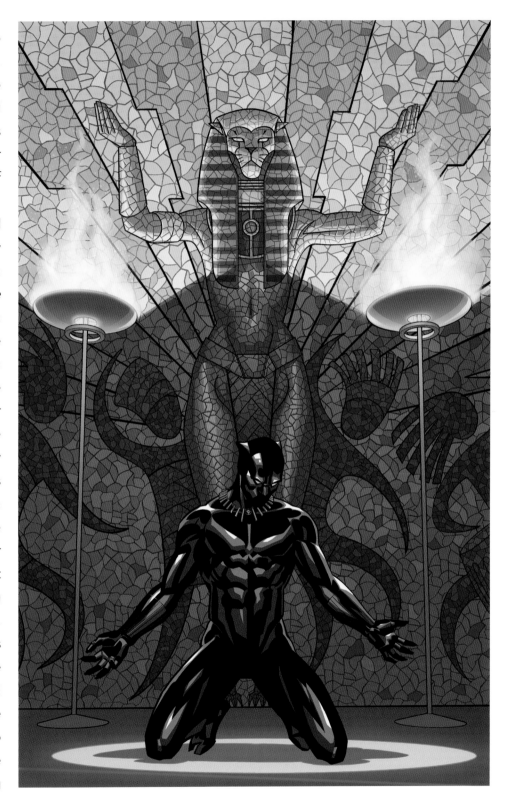

Cover art by Brian Stelfreeze for *Black Panther* #13, published April 2017.

THE WAKANDAN PROTOPIA

CHAPTER 3

Is Wakanda a real place?

That's one of the more popular questions popping up in the search-engine-verse about T'Challa's beloved nation. Although one can't point to Wakanda on a map, there's no doubt that the nation fully occupies a heartened space in the collective imagination—a land where African-born dreams will be nourished so they can grow and blossom uninterrupted; a model for harmonious systems that value the earth and its people.

The mythos is visceral and persistent. Is there a land where technology, mysticism, and nature are integrated harmoniously? Is there an African-inspired world free from the impacts of colonization? Is there an African country hiding its advanced technologies from the world? Although Wakanda inspires refreshed visions of the future, the society is taking place in the Marvel present. "Technologies aside, Wakanda is happening now," says John Jennings, comics creator and editor. "It's one of the reasons the world is so Afrofuturist."

The unconquered Wakandan empire and its technological advancements are a celestial guidepost. Depicted either in a very real East Africa near Lake Victoria, rounding the birthplace of civilization, or closer to the Democratic Republic of the Congo or Angola, Wakanda stands as the most advanced nation in the Marvel Universe. Its uninterrupted legacy of traditions and innovation are wondrous and unparalleled. Only the legend of the lost underwater world of Atlantis, a world also present in the Marvel Universe, might hold more resonance as a wistful technotopia. But where Wakanda thrives, Atlantis was first an allegory for tech gone wrong, arrogance, and gluttony that led to its destruction.

Wakanda enthusiasts know the nation lives in mind and heart, sometimes as a promise yet to be revealed, the utopia unfolding.

"T'Challa's role as a super hero is to show his Wakandan people that we can bring the best of our society, our

Brian Stelfreeze during an interview in Valencia, Spain, in 2018.

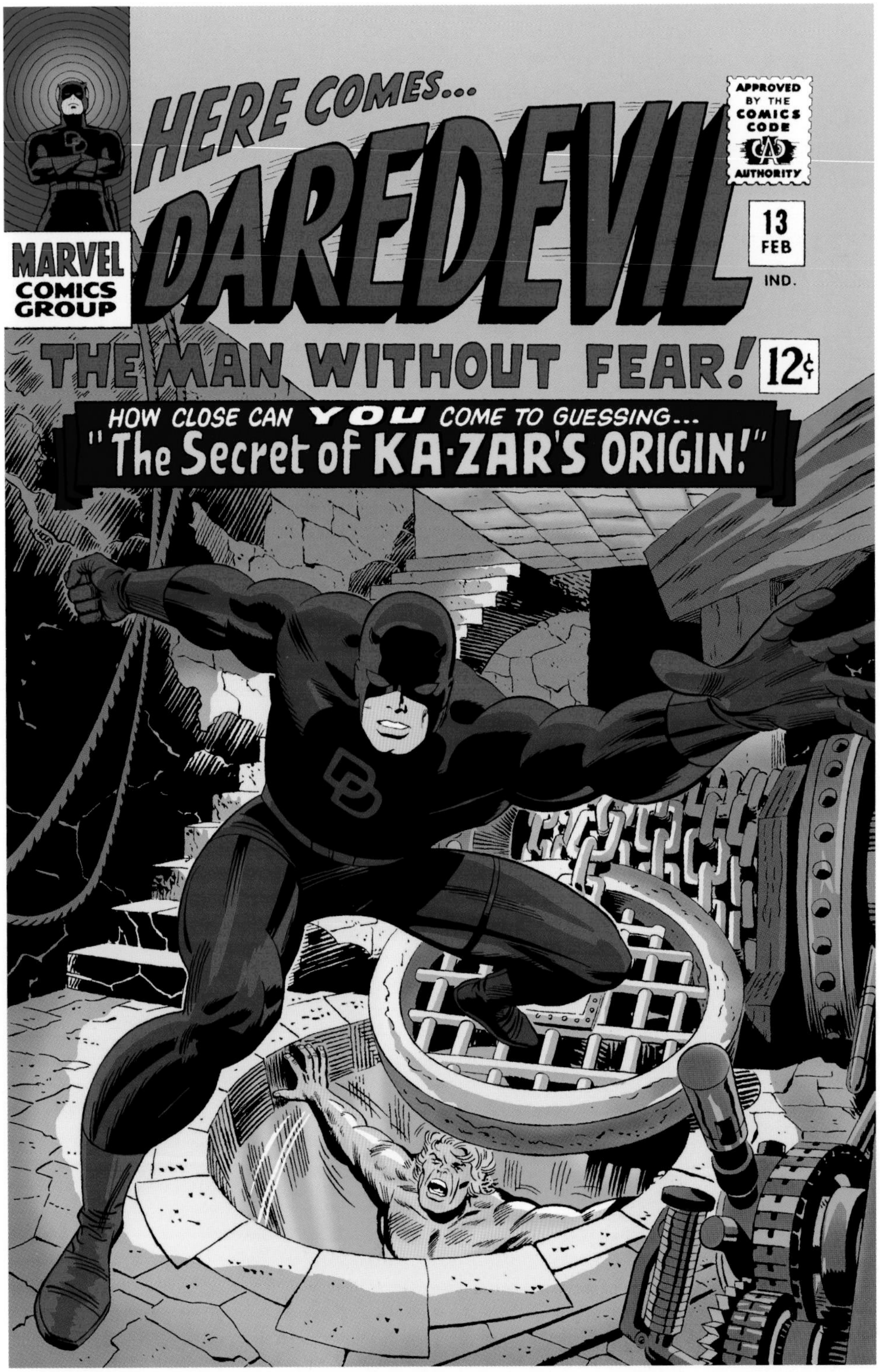
HERE COMES...
DAREDEVIL
APPROVED BY THE COMICS CODE AUTHORITY
13 FEB
IND.
MARVEL COMICS GROUP
THE MAN WITHOUT FEAR!
12¢
HOW CLOSE CAN YOU COME TO GUESSING...
"The Secret of KA-ZAR'S ORIGIN!"

The cover of *Daredevil* #13, first published February 1, 1966, which marked the first appearance of vibranium in the Marvel Comics universe.

technology, and our culture to better the world," said Evan Narcisse, writer of *Rise of the Black Panther*. "It's also to show the outside world, here's what Black ingenuity and genius can look like."

Wakanda is the only source on the planet of the meteor-spawned vibranium, a versatile (fictional) metal that holds kinetic energy. In addition to being used to create Captain America's indestructible shield, vibranium is the ultimate Wakandan power source and its most enviable resource. Vibranium is a rare metallic ore originating beyond Earth's atmosphere. It fell to Earth as a meteor. The metal has energy-manipulating properties.

Black Panther illustrator Brian Stelfreeze discussed the metal's abilities with *Popular Science* in 2016. "In the Marvel universe, vibranium has always been this material that absorbs kinetic energy," said Stelfreeze. "And any tiny bit of physics knowledge will tell you that that's really non-Newtonian. You can't just absorb energy, you've gotta change it into something else. So to the rest of the world, they only know vibranium as something that can absorb energy. But to the Wakandan scientists, they not only know that vibranium will take in energy, but they know how to get the energy back out."

Vibranium is threaded throughout Wakanda, evident in both flora and fauna. Vibranium is in Wakandan weapons and embedded in Black Panther's suit. "His suit has the technology to then recall that energy [that the vibranium absorbed]. And when it recalls it, [the suit] converts it back into kinetic energy and a little bit of waste product—photon energy, that ends up in the light show that you see," Stelfreeze said, referring to the light that bounces off Black Panther when he's in combat. "And all vibranium has this ability. When T'Challa is in his homeland, he can pull the energy of the vibranium from the ground. And it's constantly taking in energy—from footsteps to earthquakes. It gives him a little bit extra power when home, but also goes with the metaphor that he is grounded in Wakanda."

Wakadan scientific and mystical mastery of the metal fuels their technological advancements. If Wakandans didn't have exclusive access to vibranium (the nation is one of just two sites that has vibranium in the galaxy) and hadn't discovered how to adapt its powers, it's likely that the nation would not have achieved the highly esteemed position they came to hold. Their sovereignty, ability to defend themselves, way of life, and prowess are all, in part, due to Wakanda's use of the highly sought-after metal.

Jennings sees a larger symbolism within vibranium and the metal's astounding properties. "Vibranium collects and deposits sound," says Jennings. "It's an index for oral culture, hip-hop, jazz as an element."

Stelfreeze describes penciling Coates' *Black Panther* in the 2010s as one of the greatest honors of his life. While designing the relaunch, he said he wanted the comic to feel uniquely African and epic. "I don't want Wakanda to be Silicon Valley or Dubai, or anything like that," Stelfreeze told *Newsarama* in 2015. "What I want to do is show Wakanda as having technology that was created in a completely different way than technology that we know."

REALITY CHECK

Wakanda certainly feels real. The imagined space that it speaks to is as tangible as it is ethereal, a space of freedom that dreams manifest—a possibility realized, touched, and

Black Panther (2018) costume by Ruth Carter, worn in the film by Angela Bassett as Ramonda.

LEFT: *Black Panther* (2018) costume by Ruth Carter, worn in the film by Forest Whitaker as Zuri. RIGHT: Sculpture of the Black leader Zumbi dos Palmares in the historic center of the city of Salvador, Brazil.

anchored in the terra of dreamers with hard-lived experiences. The land's mythos feels so real because it overlaps with visceral cultural memory, wished-upon stars, visions, real histories, and a craving for an exemplar of African Diasporic excellence. Wakanda is both imagined and local.

Perhaps the question isn't where *is* Wakanda, but rather *when*. There are a number of historical moments

that are probable Wakandas, spaces where determined folks created idealized locales in terse worlds: Tulsa's Black Wall Street and the plethora of Black-founded American towns formed after the Civil War's end; Maroon societies like Palmares in Brazil, which held off colonizers for close to a century; or Nanny Town in Jamaica. Short-lived and potent, such moments are threaded on a larger arc of freedom. The Wakandan mythos looks back to these hard-fought dreams that didn't reach their full potentials, near-utopias undercut by bias-fueled violence.

Author Evan Narcisse was reminded of the ideals of the monumental wins of the Haitian Revolution, a war in which the enslaved freed themselves and fought off their subjugators, while writing *Rise of the Black Panther*. He thought, too, of the global punishment that followed.

"One of the realities about being Haitian American in 2018 is knowing that I come from a country that is

TOP: A scene from the Tulsa race massacre in 1921, during which white residents of the city attacked Black residents living in the Greenwood District. BOTTOM: Black residents ride in the back of a truck during the Tulsa race massacre.

A portrait of Nanny of the Maroons on Jamaican money.

poor and under-resourced by direct consequence of ousting its colonizers," he told WBUR's Christopher Lydon. "Haiti was made to pay reparations to France for the lost income it would've gotten from slavery. When I apply that to the fiction I'm writing, Wakanda is a place that never had to pay that cost. It never had to pay the cost of slavery and exploitation and it never had to pay the doubled damned cost of repayment to the colonizers.

"It's a little bittersweet when I have to think of a fantasy that embodies all that Haiti could've been without imperialism. It is bittersweet to imagine a fiction of a country that never suffered those slights while also living in a country where those slights have made a certain kind of injustice prevalent for people like me."

Martin R. Delany, renaissance man and second to Frederick Douglass in late nineteenth-century influence, published a speculative fiction series of stories about a post-slavery society. *Blake, or the Huts of America* saw Cuba as a destination for freed slaves. The stories ran in the *Anglo-African American* magazine and the *Weekly Anglo-African* in 1859 through 1862. The idea of a post-slavery society with self-determination infused discourse among Black people in the Americas.

"Marcus Garvey was talking about a United States of Africa at the beginning of the twentieth century," said

Claire A. Nelson, founder of the Futures Forum. Nelson studies futures for African Americans and sees Wakanda as a long-standing idea in progress. She notes that both Liberia and Sierra Leone were attempts of the formerly enslaved from the US and elsewhere to create new societies that were complex and undermined. She compares the Rastafarian saying "Down with Babylon, up with Zion" as a Biblical-inspired call for the idealistic space that Wakanda has come to symbolize. The Rastafarians, originally formed in Jamaica, looked to Ethiopia, Africa's uncolonized nation, as inspiration for this Zion. "Wakanda is certainly an emotional place," said Nelson. "That's why it caught on. We know it. We want this place to exist so we can go there to escape, even if it's just in our minds."

AM I WAKANDAN?

One of the more fascinating evolutions in the surge of Black Panther fandom is the cultural touchstone that T'Challa's homeland has become, with some fans arguing over which society the fictive nation approximates. "It's that hidden story of the true story of Africa and the greatness of the civilizations that were there," said Sista Zai Zanda, an Afrofuturist storyteller born in Zimbabwe and currently living in Australia. "The popular image of Africa that's out there

Martin R. Delany.

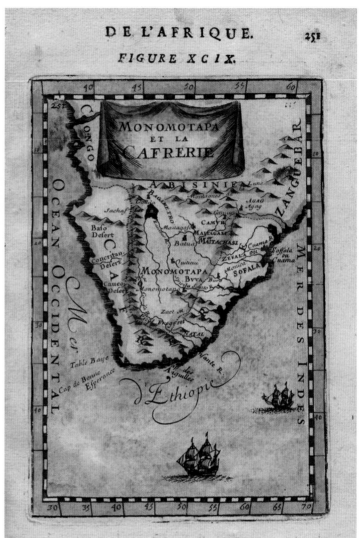

LEFT: Chadwick Boseman attends the 2018 MTV Movie and TV Awards. RIGHT: A 1719 map of the Mutapa Empire.

is not one that we grow up with. When I look at it from the standpoint of the diaspora, surrounded by second-generation Africans in Australia who are in spaces where they are told they are inferior, Wakanda is an affirmation of self, an affirmation of greatness."

Chadwick Boseman, who played T'Challa in Marvel Studios' *Black Panther*, believed that Wakanda was an amalgamation of prosperous ancient African nations of the past. Wakanda is "the Mutapa empire of fifteenth-century Zimbabwe," he said in the *New York Times*. "Wakanda is the stargazing kingdom of the Dogon. There are many things you can fuse together here, many rulers and warriors

throughout world history that your imagination can draw from at any given moment."

Author and Egyptian history enthusiast Anthony T. Browder is convinced that Wakanda is the Ancient Egyptian city of Waset, also known as Luxor. Waset was capital of Egypt during the Middle and New Kingdom, home to Hatshepsut's 90-foot obelisk towers and the Luxor Temple. It is heralded as one of history's greatest civilizations. "It could've been an inspiration," said Lucarelli. "The city had many large temples and tombs. I like that association."

Much of twentieth-century African American art and lore referenced Ancient Egypt and Nubia as an idealized height of human achievement to return to. Ancient Egypt was celebrated as a high-level African society of the past whose ways and impact were ones to aspire to or recreate. In some ways, Ancient Egypt occupied the imagined, aspirational space that Wakanda does for some today: an African society whose ways aren't entirely understood but who had a mastery of their resources and the esoteric.

Entrance of the Luxor Temple, Egypt.

Sphinx of Hatshepsut, on display at the
Metropolitan Museum of Art in New York.

Everything from the principles of Maat to the recreationist practices in honor of Egyptian gods proliferate African American culture. Ancient Egypt's impact on Greek and Roman empires, both pillars of Western thought, couldn't be denied. The old world has the new world captivated, so much so that for years some scholars and film depictions didn't want to acknowledge the country was comprised of people of color, most of whom would be described as Black today. Music artists including Sun Ra, Charles Earland, Earth, Wind & Fire, Erykah Badu, Kamasi Washington, and Janelle Monáe hail Egyptian inspirations as a reclamation of erased Black histories projected into futures. Ancient Egypt symbolized greatness, excellence, the heights of achievement, wealth, mastery of intellect, science, and mysticism.

SO WAKANDA IS REAL?

"Wakanda is not a fantasy. The Mali empire, the Songhay empire, Oyo empire. There's the Benin Kingdom that had walls that were miles longer than the Great Walls of China," said Nigerian speculative fiction writer Oghenechovwe Donald Ekpeki. "Wakanda is not such a novelty. The idea of an independent-run African kingdom, it existed before it was interrupted. Mansa Musa was one of the wealthiest men in history."

LEFT: The obelisk of Hatshepsut. RIGHT: Relief of
the lion-headed god Apedemak in Sudan.

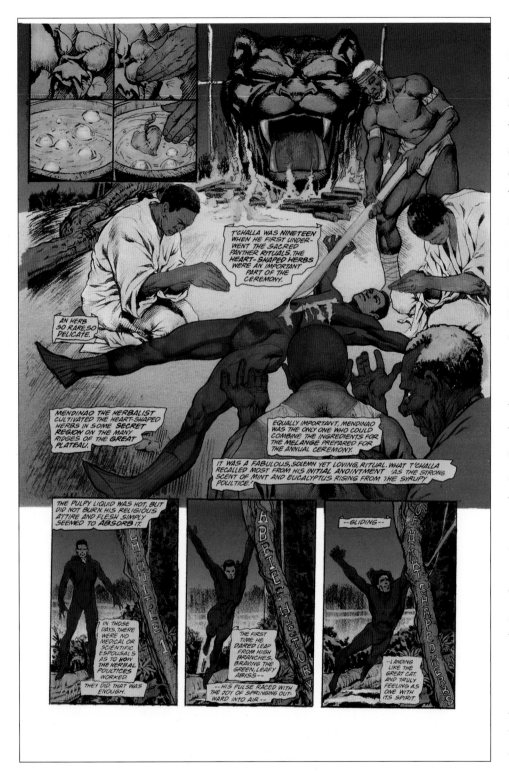

The Heart-Shaped Herb is used in the ritual to pass on the Black Panther's powers to a new protector of Wakanda, as seen in *Fantastic Four* #52 in July 1966.

Ekpeki said that for many Africans living in Africa, Wakanda isn't the dream to move to, but rather a reframing of advanced societies of the past. "On the continent, Wakanda reminds us of a past modern future. It's more like we did that already, then this is our future. These things are not imaginings, but reimaginings, which is also okay." Lest one forget, many African nations have royal courts, monarchies, and the politics that come with it. Ekpeki even noted that vigilantes who help fight crime also exist in parts of Nigeria too. "Wakanda is familiar," he said.

As for the magical elements in the story—the Heart-Shaped Herb, the ancestor realms, conversing with deities—these, too, are cultural. "The average African has slight issues with fantasy and magic realism because a lot of those things aren't fantasy, they are culture, they are religion," said Ekpeki. "A lot of it is real stuff that we live with or grow up with. There are people who practice the African Traditional Religions like juju or jazz in Nigeria."

Ethiopia stands proud as the only African nation to ward off colonizers, fending off an invasion by Italy. They, too, point to a supernatural and treasured natural resource, the mythic Ark of the Covenant. Their lion of Judah and the lion-headed god Apademak of Kush could be a distant cousin to Black Panther. Ethiopia's crowning achievement inspired the Rastafarian movement in Jamaica where King Haile Selassie is recrafted as a god-king.

Ethiopian Prince Joel Makonnen recently co-authored an Afrofuturist book, *Last Gate of the Emperor*, with Kwame Mbalia. Inspired by childhood stories and histories of his homeland, the story takes place in a futuristic Addis Ababa and follows a teen gamer with an active imagination who embarks on a galactic quest to find his uncle and ultimately his origins.

"The research I needed to do was in my heart and in my memory because these are stories that I grew up with," he told *Scifipost.com*. "What surprised me is how little people in the West, especially in America, know about Ethiopian legacy. With such a long history going back thousands of years, I'm surprised by how more people are familiar with the Roman Empire, British monarchy, and the Greeks. As I learn more about my country, I'm also always fascinated by how many incredible feats we have achieved as a nation."

"Until fairly recently, 'Afrofuturism' has been an untapped genre," Makonnen said. "I wanted to contribute to it, because I want my family's legacy and history to continue into the future." In one sense, Wakanda has become shorthand for writing about African worlds in the future and past, particularly for Western audiences who

Haile Selassie, Emperor of Ethiopia, circa 1924.

The Lion of Judah.

are just beginning to see these enriched takes more frequently. The success of *Black Panther* as a film and its commercial viability made it easier for Afrofuturist and Black speculative fiction writers to share these stories with the world. Moreover, the success of the comic, especially as the film led more people to Black Panther stories, became an example to follow. Both the film and the comics ultimately worked in tandem to affirm a demand for stories about African heroes in Africa and Black characters in sci-fi and fantasy globally.

Ekpeki is one of the most decorated Black speculative fiction writers in Africa. He compared his award-winning novella *Ife-Iyoku, the Tale of Imadeyunuagbon*, a future imagining of the Oya Empire, as "Wakanda in reverse" where "everyone is a T'Challa."

WAKANDA BEFORE AMERICA

Although Wakanda's mythos goes to the root of freedom dreams and prosperous ancient African empires, its esoteric leanings may have a distinctly American Indigenous influence too. *Wakanda*—Wah'Kon-Tah—has Native American origins. The word is used by the Omaha, the Kansa, the Onka, and the Osage, among others, as a name for God that also means "the mysterious." It also doubled as an altered reality or ancestor realm. Reports as early as 1873 identified Wah'Kon-Tah as being both "a source and a destination: a place from which all goodness emerged and to which all aspired to journey."

"I remember reading the comic as a kid and remember my mind being blown that it was used," Newton Cass, an Osage tribal member, told *Indian Country*. "I always thought that it was used

appropriately, being that we all come from the Creator, and it was used in that context."

Wrote Peter Manseau in the *Washington Post*, "It's useful to remember that among those who first used the word [Wakanda], it served as shorthand for the hope of a place beyond such conflicts. By definition, Wakanda was a concept whose reality could not be limned in the usual ways. As long-ago ethnographers explained, 'Each person thought in his heart that Wakanda existed.'"

A Black family leaving Florida during the Great Depression.

MY LITTLE WAKANDA

Aspects of African American life can be seen as proxies to Wakanda and life in that nation. HBCUs, the Harlem Renaissance, Chicago during the Great Migration, Black suburban communities, and cultural centers have all been

Black people traveling from New Orleans disembark at Union Station in Chicago during the Great Migration, circa 1953.

discussed in the context of being Wakandan spaces or Wakandan moments in time. In these cases, Wakanda is a metaphor for nurturing environments where creativity, freedom, and innovation are supported. "Any place where we can be liberated, Black, and free could be a Wakandan space," said Jennings.

When Phillip Beckham, founder of the Mid-South Business Association and Resource Center (MSBARC), a community economic development organization, called his childhood neighborhood in Harvey, Illinois, Wakanda, he was not speaking about innovation. "My neighborhood in Harvey, every house had a father," he said, recalling the Black family networks, the caring teachers in his all-Black school, and the high expectations and discipline. "When I saw the [Black Panther] movie, I realized, we were living in our own little Wakanda."

"I grew up in Zimbabwe in the '80s and '90s and that was Wakanda," said Zanda. "We had folks from all over the continent. You have so much culture, so much music, it's alive," she said, reflecting on the economic prosperity and cultural abundance of the time. "You could be in your beingness without having to be anyone else to get ahead," said Zanda. She felt the same way when her family visited an HBCU in the US. These moments have resounding impact.

"[Wakanda] is a fictional construct but it's a fictional construct filled with the construct of decades of self-reliance, self-love, and survival," says Narcisse.

For Taylor Witten, Wakanda symbolized the nexus of community and creativity. "Our community was thirsting for a community where we could play," she said. Witten was so taken by the lore of Wakanda that she co-produced a fan con in homage to T'Challa's homeland. Wakandacon was a three-day, family-friendly event designed to "celebrate the Black community, STEM, creativity, and pop culture all through the lens of Black Panther." Rapper Drunken Monkeee, named for the martial arts fighting style

Smalls Paradise, a Harlem nightclub.

Ryan Coogler attends a *Black Panther* (2018)
screening at the Brooklyn Academy of Music on
February 14, 2018.

(his alias is M'Baku, after the Black Panther character), sought to create a similar day of family fun with Chi-Kanda, a kid-friendly event with battle dancing, hip-hop performances, and Black history quizzes.

The Wakanda Effect was a term popularized after the success of Marvel Studios' *Black Panther* to describe the impact of audiences seeing the Black utopian world. Interest in Wakanda accelerated the interest in Afrofuturist visions of the future. Wakanda's reimagining, buoyed by the film, inspired a rethinking of hopeful futures that celebrated STEM, fashion, and reflections on African and African Diasporic values. The what-if scenarios posed by the Wakandan lore and fast-forwarded with the success of the film were far-reaching. Walter Gleason, a New Jersey–based professor, and Reynaldo Anderson, professor and founder of the Black Speculative Arts Movement (BSAM), created a Wakanda syllabus to explore historical markers, themes, and world-building within the Wakandan realm.

Futurists caught on. "Wisdom From Wakanda: Five Transportation Insights From 'Black Panther'" appeared in *Forbes*. Reports of singer Akon's proposed crypto, high-tech city in Senegal was described as the makings of a "real-life Wakanda." Other articles speculated on minerals that had vibranium-like properties. There are some developers even looking to build an African city and name it after Marvel's vibranium-rich nation.

UTOPIA IN QUESTION

Wakanda is a self-governed African nation and a competitive player on the Marvel Universe's world stage, revered in both the fictional reality and ours for its might, versatility, progressive gender politics, traditions, and innovation. Wakanda controls its resources, which they've harnessed to create a prosperous society, and advanced technologies

fuel everything from transportation to medicine. The protection of Bast and their mastery of vibranium makes them undefeatable. Even their economy rebounds quickly. In the comic, Wakanda is guided by ideals it supersedes more often than it fails, taking pride in exceptionalism. Frankly, they are the envy of the Marvel world.

"Wakanda is about exceptionalism and Black excellence," said Stanford Carpenter. For some, Wakanda has become a personal gold standard for performance.

"It's about being the best or better than the rest," said Carpenter, adding that there's a hint of respectability politics in the world's framing. WVON Radio host Art "Chat Daddy" Sims once jokingly speculated with his show's guests about a trip to Wakanda, noting that they wouldn't all be allowed to enter. "Some of y'all just aren't ready," he said, as if entering Wakanda was akin to a gateway to heaven or a VIP luxury vacation package. Entering the fabled world, among other things, required a health-conscious vegan diet, upstanding morals, a sense of African-inspired style, and acceptable behavior, he said. This notion of who can enter and who can't gave rise to the dynamics of a Black Utopia and what it meant in practice.

A NATION UNDER SIEGE

Just as Black Panther is always several steps ahead, the nation he leads is light-years ahead of the rest (including Marvel's Atlantis) in its integration of mysticism, technology, and ethics. However, even uncolonized worlds with great intentions can have their faults. Much of the comic's later iterations explore the nature of power, legacy, myth, royalty, and the conflicts of ruling an empire.

"Black Panther is about trying to keep the balance between the ancestral realm and the human world," said Zanda. "When leadership is steeped in African

The first on-panel appearance of Misty Knight, in *Marvel Premiere* #21, published March 10, 1975.

spirituality, you have an obligation that extends beyond. There's no separation of the human and spirit, so to govern everything has to be balanced across all planes." Nature, technology, humans, animal life, and governing must be centered around a valuing of life and existence. "Every society had those principles," she said. "When we don't, we go down a colonial path."

Until the Black Panther's debut on the Marvel stage, Wakanda hid in plain sight. An uncolonized African nation with uninterrupted cultural and technological development, led by an even-tempered genius king who doubles as a super hero empowered by an Egyptian goddess, was presented as a bit of a shocker when it was first referenced in the *Fantastic Four* in the mid-'60s. Throughout Black Panther's history, Wakanda's advancements made it an unparalleled sovereign power in the Marvel Universe and a probable danger in waiting. Yet, Wakanda's isolationist practices, while heroic, present a quandary with respect to what it's fighting for. Wakanda as counternarrative to colonial impact on African spaces undergirds the utopian sensibility. Wakanda for Wakandans is rooted in a justified mistrust of the world that T'Challa tries to move his kingdom away from.

"When [T'Challa] fights to become king, he's fighting for the ideals that have kept Wakanda uncolonized for decades," Narcisse told *Radio Open Source* with Christopher Lydon on WBUR Boston. "Those ideas are self-determination, Black agency, and Black glory of living in defiance of the kind of exploitation that ruined the rest of the continent of Africa. Colonization and imperialism took T'Challa's dad from him."

T'Challa becomes this bridge for the African Diaspora and African Continent, fighting the supernatural while establishing a base in Harlem with a Kingdom Wakanda and later a galactic planet in space. In addition to his role with the Avengers, he builds relationships with Luke Cage, Blade, Misty Knight, and members of the Crew in part to address issues plaguing urban America.

However, once the nation's powers are revealed, an occurrence that happens with Black Panther's debut, Wakanda is constantly under threat. Wakandan tech achievements attracted as many enemies as they did curious parties. Nemesis Ulysses S. Klaw wreaked havoc on the nation's stability, befriending and killing T'Challa's father, in hopes of stealing the nation's vibranium. He stoked anti-Wakandan vengeance in T'Challa's most personally conflicted foe, Killmonger, and set the stage for T'Challa's deeper wrestling with upholding legacy.

The Black Panther and Ulysses Klaw clash again in *Black Panther* #166, published October 25, 2017.

Ulysses Klaw first appears in *Fantastic* Four #53, published August 1966.

Although Wakanda is respected on the Marvel world stage, it still stands as a relative mystery among its global counterparts. CIA officer Everett K. Ross is charged with keeping tabs on young King T'Challa and his whereabouts, largely because of Wakanda's mysteriousness. Ross' inability to truly grasp the Wakandan world, its mysticism, or T'Challa's heroic actions didn't change drastically even when Ross temporarily became head of the African nation during T'Challa's astral travels. Ross' verbal fumbles as he tried to relay the death-defying feats of Black Panther to authorities are a tongue-in-cheek commentary on Western misunderstandings of African nations, and Black people in general.

Even the Dora Milaje, as a mighty, all-women, indefatigable military arm, challenge all conventions of power and gender and are also highly respected curiosities by non-Wakandans. Their ways are unknown to outsiders and they like it that way. Wakanda is not to be messed with. It is mightier and, much like its leader, smarter than everyone else. The nation doesn't seek to rule over other nations, prioritizing the well-being of its people and its sovereignty above all else. Their power, wealth, and achievements make them the envy of the world. They have intelligence agents everywhere, including in the outer realms and on Mars. Wakanda is a staunch ally in the Avengers' adventures despite the fact that T'Challa's initial interest in joining was in part to spy on them too.

Coates' *A Nation Under Our Feet* questions T'Challa's monarchy as the freedom dream and gives rise to the nation's delicate shift to a young democracy—a democracy made up of tense, sometimes polarizing, factions. Whether the story is more a commentary on American exceptionalism, the politics of African rule, or the short-sightedness of revolutionaries can be debated. The politics of a utopia, even a Black nation, necessitate that someone must be on the bottom, and T'Challa's rule as monarch is dismantled in favor of a Wakanda where all can participate. This questioning of the nature of monarchy, and the shifting of power for T'Challa, made some fans upset. Can you still be a Black super hero without absolute power? Can a king who's no longer king in a world that wades into the mundaneness of democracy align with the fantasy?

"Wakanda can extract without exploiting. The places that want to attack want to extract and exploit," said Zanda. "Democracy becomes about how to manage power; however, the lust for power can overtake how to govern intelligently and wisely."

The exploration of Wakanda as myth and practice has inspired an array of discussions about world building. What does the ideal society, one that values humanity, nature,

Ulysses Klaw battles the Fantastic Four on the cover of *Fantastic Four* #56, published November 1, 1966.

and the Earth look like? Wakanda, when it lives up to the best idea of itself, can be that. However, living the myth into reality, and upholding the expectations of the ancestors, while balancing a new world and compensating for the ancestors' faults, becomes an all-consuming juggling act for T'Challa. T'Challa may be a caretaker for an ideal that he alone cannot exact.

With his run on the series, Coates sought to dismantle ideas of Black monarchies and all Black worlds as being inherently aspirational or idealistic. Practices, policies, and a system of checks and balances were essential to value all people in any society that lays claims to exceptionalism, including Wakanda. "Wakanda's the most advanced country in the world, with a really educated population. Why would they even accept a monarchy?" Coates asked.

NEW WORLDS, NEW VISIONS

Futurist and digital nomad Monika Bielskyte is a Black Panther fan, but she's not a fan of utopias or dystopias as a binary proxy for world-building. Utopias can raise the question of who, exactly, they are utopias for when class stratifications exist, while dystopias, even cyberpunk sexy ones, can foster hopelessness. Bielskyte prefers thinking of Wakanda as an Afrofuturist protopia, a possibility in an array of futures that values humanity, nonexploitative practices, and the Earth. She often uses Wakanda as an example of a sci-fi world with healthy, indigenous practices to model for new futures. "We can be scientifically advanced but we can still make sure the living world is thriving with the rivers, land, and rituals." Her research project, Protopia Futures, is a borderless collective that developed a framework for model futures inspired by innovators at the "forefront of Black feminism and Indigenous, Queer and Disability activism."

"Protopia is centered around seven principles. In my talks I use Wakanda as an illustration of one of the only mainstream sci-fi narratives that reflects most protopian ideas. It didn't reflect all the aspects of protopia but there are some that are key to inclusive future visioning," she said. Those points include a society with plurality beyond binaries, community beyond borders, celebration of presence, regenerative action, and life as technology, as well as creativity and emergent subcultures.

"Wakanda has different types of people from different regions and yet they formed a cohesive whole. Even where there's monarchy there was a story and a narrative around people coming together," said Bielskyte. "When community doesn't come together, that's when the tragedy happens." Wakanda isn't heteronormative in gender depictions. There's an intergenerational presence. A protopian hero isn't an individual but a community itself.

"In a lot of sci-fi, people are lonely with their technology, looking at a polluted skyline. But there's joy and a notion of being present in Wakanda," said Bielskyte. "They have all this fancy technology but they aren't lost in some virtual world. They are embodied, they are dancing, hugging each other, and physically being in the world." Even when they talk about plant technology in the form of the Heart-Shaped Herb, it's not about escape or simulation but getting closer to one another and life, she reasoned.

Even the nature of how Wakanda thinks about power is protopian. When T'Challa's people demand democracy, after some assessment, he agrees to it as he tries to reconcile with his new role. "T'Challa and his family don't seem to be concerned with being the richest. They're more concerned with how we live or exist in a world that has a very different knowledge system than ours," Bielskyte said.

"Even the goodies in some stories are simply resisting the bad forces. Their identity is shaped around fighting the evil. But they don't necessarily reflect the good. In Wakanda, to have power is to have responsibilities, it's not just to exert violent force on others. Wakanda is not just based on defending itself against the evil world it's in opposition to. It's proactive in creating what is meaningful," said Bielskyte.

In *Intergalactic Empire of Wakanda*, when T'Challa must defeat a new world order on a sister planet founded by Wakandans, it's demonstrated that even the most well-intentioned society, a galaxy removed, can evolve into a tyrannical dictatorship. This interstellar Wakanda, technological heights aside, is not Wakanda at its best. T'Challa witnesses this firsthand as one in the world's lower rungs, during his rise from enslavement on Planet Bast to claiming his place in the new world, where everyone is named after the legends of his lifetime. The story alludes to the experience of enslaved Africans and the role of myth in their survival while asserting that their resilience is tantamount to myth itself.

"In this Wakanda, I was not just a king, I was a mythical hero," says T'Challa. "And what was a hero without his trials?" He later confides his insights to Storm. "No nation on my shoulders, no ancestral past. And I discovered that this was the real labor, this was the trial, to find myself not just amongst my lineage, but also cut off from it."

Variant cover artwork for *Black Panther: The Sound and the Fury* #1, published February 2018.

A variant cover for *Black Panther* #1, published May 2018, by Yasmine Putri.

Lonny J. Avi Brooks had been thinking of creating an imagination forecasting game that centered nonwhite worlds. A professor of strategic communications at California State University, East Bay, his first foray was a card game based on Wakanda, called Wakanda Visions. In the game, players could go to different areas of Wakanda and solve problems. The exploration was a practice tool for what later evolved into Afro-Rithms from the Future.

"I realized that these imagination forecasting games are very generic because they're trying to appeal to such a wide audience," Brooks said. "So, I started coming up with different kinds of tensions in the future. Will there be more or less African innovation in the tension? Will there be more or less AI in the future? Will there be Black storytelling in the future? We pick two cards, and use those tensions to build a scenario.

"I was brainstorming the game when I came across these artworks on Broadway and 9th in Oakland. The panels said, 'Welcome to Panther Territory' and included fantastic images inspired by Wakanda and social justice work. The art was created by Terica Lewis, former Black Panther Party leader who was instrumental in the creation of the breakfast program.

"It was a sign to keep going," said Brooks. Afro-Rithms has become one of the foremost games of its kind. The game has been played at futures training workshops for UNESCO, SXSW, the Stanford Design School, and tech teams at Google, among others, and featured in the *Atlantic* and the *Guardian*.

After the players vote on the two tensions to utilize for world building, they are handed another set of cards (system cards, inspiration cards, and object cards) to create an artifact of the future. "For example, we came up with Angela Davis shoes, where you can walk with Angela Davis and you're walking in Oakland and holographic images of the Black Panther party come up," said Brooks. "It's about how can we think out of the box,

there are no wrong answers, and we create a safe space." Brooks formalized the game with Eli Kosminsky and Ahmed Best, who is perhaps best known for portraying Jar Jar Binks in the *Star Wars* prequel trilogy.

Afro-Rithms has a virtual counterpart and is central to the Community Futures School, which Brooks founded at the Museum of Children's Arts, in Downtown Oakland. "What if we had marginalized people who showcase part of their visions of the future, as part of a regional world's fair of community visions? LGBTQ visions, Arab visions, Chinese visions, Indigenous visions, African visions that get showcased and can lay the foundation for community-based programming and legislative agendas."

He debuted the game at the Institute for the Future in Palo Alto. "It was a wonderland of Afrofuturist," said Brooks. "Among the first artifacts suggested was a tattoo that when waved by an ATM released funds for reparations. The goal is to give people agency that they can be signals of change. The other is to create artifacts that could become prototypes for actual products."

Whether as future modeling or a past reasserted, aspiration or alternate dimension, Wakanda's reality is multilayered. There seem to be systems within Wakandan culture that ensure it returns to its ideals, which is inspiring for new futures. Wakanda is bigger than its thoughtful monarch in transition. It may be bigger than the story itself. Yet, Wakanda's realness does not waver.

"Although it's mythical and mystical, it's real," said Dr. Claire Nelson, Chief Ideation Leader with the Futures Forum, of Wakanda. "It doesn't make it less real. It's as real as Babylon in the Bible. Wakanda has entered the lexicon for Black people in the Americas." And it's part of the lexicon for many people shaping new, livable futures today.

A concept illustration of the ancestral plane, created by Vance Kovacs for *Black Panther* (2018).

THE MODERN GODDESS & FUTURISTIC WARRIOR QUEENS

To call the women of Wakanda resident badasses is an understatement. Known for their strength, intelligence, valor, love of community, and loyalty to the Wakandan ideal, they've been elevated as respected icons and archetypes. In Wakanda, being a woman isn't a barrier to leadership, becoming a monarch, running the new democracy, leading a rebellion, becoming an orisha (or deity/spirit), or taking on the role of Black Panther. It doesn't go unnoticed that the Dora Milaje, Storm, and Shuri don't downplay themselves to be in T'Challa's orbit. Nor does T'Challa in his recent iterations expect them to. The Dora Milaje are fierce warriors, as strong and capable as the king they defend—and their power reigns without the help of the sought-after Heart-Shaped Herb, the source of Black Panther's super hero powers. Anyone can have the title of Black Panther, a title that Shuri bore with the pride akin to her brother's. The undeterred wit and might of these women wields a weighted blow to the problematic characterizations of Black women both past and present.

"Black girls are very excited to see Black women and Black girls as super heroes and protectors," said Kelly Fair, founder of Polished Pebbles, a girl's mentoring organization. Shuri is a shapeshifting scientist, the Dora Milaje are compassionate warriors, Folasade is the vigilant prime minister, Queen Ramonda is a wise advisor to her son, and N'Yami, T'Challa's birth mother, was one of the top scientists of her time. "I don't know any girls who saw the women in Wakanda and said, 'oh that would never happen' or 'girls don't do that,'" Fair said. "I'm almost comfortable in saying they felt like this is who we are."

"Girls today feel comfortable being fierce," said Fair. Black Panther helps them see themselves as heroes. "They see the idea of being a defender of freedom as a natural goal," said Fair.

GROWING PAINS

The women in Wakanda are arguably some of the most complex and multifaceted women in the Marvel Universe. Their symbolism as smart and savvy defenders is preeminent. However, this take on Wakanda's female citizens is an evolution and clear departure from some of their pre-2005 renditions. At one point, the formidable Dora Milaje were the royal ladies-in-waiting, a fighting squad of barely legal women who could only speak to the king. Nakia and Okoye, known for their leadership and battle

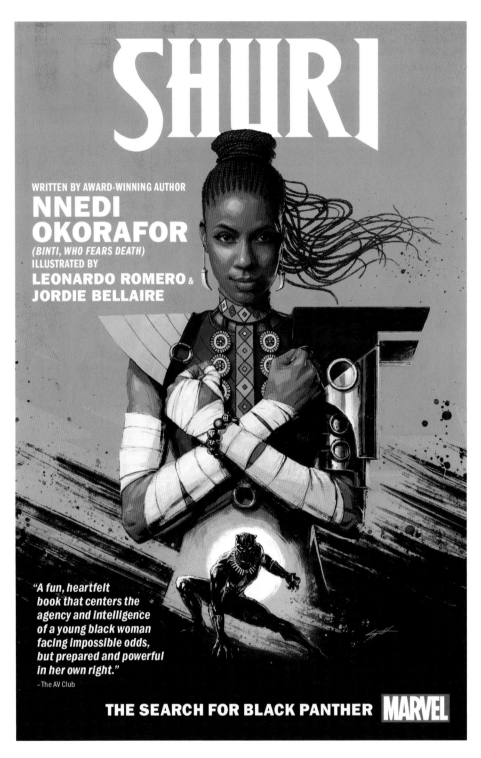

SHURI

WRITTEN BY AWARD-WINNING AUTHOR
NNEDI OKORAFOR
(BINTI, WHO FEARS DEATH)
ILLUSTRATED BY
LEONARDO ROMERO &
JORDIE BELLAIRE

"A fun, heartfelt book that centers the agency and intelligence of a young black woman facing impossible odds, but prepared and powerful in her own right."
- The AV Club

THE SEARCH FOR BLACK PANTHER **MARVEL**

The trade paperback cover of *Shuri Vol 1: The Search for Black Panther*, published April 24, 2019, which collects issues #1–5 of Shuri's first ongoing series.

Roxane Gay in Los Angeles, California, in 2019.

skill today, were originally vixens adept at combat in long tresses and stilettos. Nakia, sometimes dubbed the fallen Dora, became so obsessed with T'Challa and his lack of romantic interest that she evolved into the vindictive nemesis Malice, an enraged woman hell-bent on the demise of her former boss.

Moreover, a litany of tragedy beset women who got too close to T'Challa in the comics. Monica Lynne, an African American singer and T'Challa's first fiancé, helped him defeat the racist Sons of the Serpent as a socially conscious victor. Their engagement was short-lived (T'Challa is forever married to Wakanda) and yet, after their breakup,

she fell into the hands of his enemies, the violated pawn for the menacing Klaw and other foes who kidnapped the songstress to lure out the king. Malice, in a fit of jealousy, once tossed her from a flying plane.

Queen Ramonda, T'Challa's stepmother, was abducted by white supremacist Anton Pretorius and was abused for years. But the assumption at the time was that the queen had simply left Wakanda to be with another man. When T'Challa learned otherwise, years later, he finally rescued her.

The damsel in distress, consummate victim, jealous lover, and combat-ready vixen defaults were common before the early 2000s. Yet there were outspoken characters—like the American-reared Dora Milaje, poet

Queen Divine Justice, and Monica Lynne, in Christopher Priest and Don McGregor's runs, respectively—that forged dimension. Still, most of the more popular women in Wakanda were created at the onset of the new millennium. "Okoye was created in '98. Shuri was created in the 2000s. Oyo was created in the last ten years," said comics journalist and author Angélique Roché. The characters' evolutions can't be ignored.

Reginald Hudlin most notably added Shuri and Storm to Black Panther's story, crafting Shuri's path to the Black Panther mantle. Ta-Nehisi Coates yearned to explore the Wakandan world and was instrumental in recruiting the first women and nonbinary writers to pen Wakandan tales. Roxane Gay wrote the *World of Wakanda* series and Nnedi Okorafor and Vita Ayala penned a self-titled series for Shuri in 2018.

"Roxane wanted to know who these women are," said Roché. "She wanted to know where did they come from? How did they get to this point?" Gay's love story between Ayo and Aneka, members of the Midnight Angels, a Dora Milaje elite fighting squad, explores the women's intense romance and their growing mistrust of the monarchy.

"Ultimately, it was a thrill to write a super hero and rethink who can be heroic and why," said Gay. "It was also a

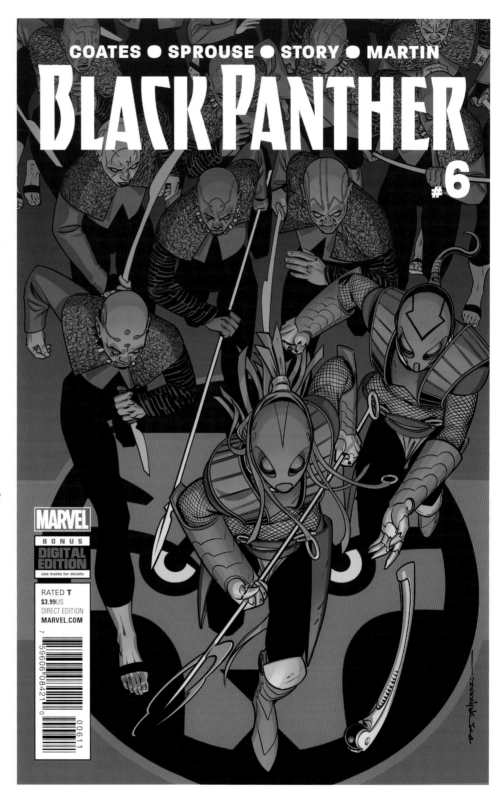

COATES ● SPROUSE ● STORY ● MARTIN
BLACK PANTHER
#6

MARVEL
BONUS
DIGITAL EDITION
see inside for details

RATED T
$3.99 US
DIRECT EDITION
MARVEL.COM

The Dora Milaje on the cover of *Black Panther* #6, published September 2016.

A group of retired Dahomey warriors, 1908.

thrill to imagine super heroes motivated by more than their own traumas, not that there's anything wrong with that."

Okorafor and Ayala highlighted the complications of Shuri's journey, one where newfound shapeshifting powers and an ability to connect with the ancestral plane primed her for leadership in Wakanda in her brother's absence. Okorafor also humanized the maligned Malice.

Roché dubs the small number of women writers, letterers, and illustrators—including letterer Janice Chang, colorist Glynis Wein, and Alysa Martinez, who illustrated Marvel Knights—as the real women of Wakanda. "These women brought these characters to life," she says.

However, no one can underestimate the impact of Marvel Studios' Black Panther on popularizing Shuri as a young genius scientist and the Dora Milaje as the ultimate fighting squad in pop culture consciousness.

AMAZONS TO DORA MILAJE

The Amazons of Greek lore may have been the first all-women fighting army to enter the Western mythos. When French invaders descended upon the Dahomey empire, now in modern-day Benin in West Africa, they described the thousands of women warriors they faced as the legendary Amazons come to life. Formed in the seventeenth century, the Dahomey all-women army was sworn to the king's protection, fighting colonizers, and toppling neighboring kingdoms as they expanded and defended their empire. Fighting with sickles that could slice a man in half, the women were notoriously vicious fighters. Although there are other warrior queens who were the Dahomean's contemporaries, including Nzinga of Matamba (modern-day Angola) who led armies in battle, the Dahomey were the only ethnic group that had women warriors who numbered in the thousands. A French marine, Monrienval, was utterly shocked by the army's fighting capabilities. "[Neither] the cannon nor the canister shot, nor the salvo fire stops them," he said, according to the *Amazons of Black Sparta: The Women*

Colorized illustration (after a nineteenth-century drawing) of Nzinga of Matamba.

A Dahomey warrior, circa 1890.

Warriors of Dahomey. It's likely that the Dahomey army inspired the Dora Milaje's evolution.

Despite their heroic feats, the Dahomey army, known as the Agojie, have a complicated past. They were feared, revered, vilified, mighty, and terrifying. Some were prisoners of war and others were volunteers. Although they valiantly fought off colonizers, they were also used by their leaders to wage war against other African kingdoms with the aim of selling captives into the transatlantic slave trade. "More perhaps than any other African state, Dahomey was dedicated to warfare and slave-raiding," said Stanley B. Alpern in the book *Amazons of Black Sparta.* People in the Dahomey Kingdom were sold into the trade, as well, with women in the Agojie likely among them.

In 1927, writer Zora Neale Hurston interviewed Cudjo Lewis, a formerly enslaved man who was aboard the last ship of human cargo to come to the US. His account was included in Hurston's book, *Barracoon: The Story of the Last Black Cargo,* which wasn't published until 2020. Lewis, who was eighty-six at the time of his interview, provided one of the few firsthand accounts on record by a survivor of the Middle Passage, recounting that he was a teenager when his village was ransacked and he was kidnapped. In his explicit account, he identified the Dahomey all-women army as the culprit.

Hippolyte, the father of Haitian Revolution leader Toussaint Louverture and an aristocrat in the Allada kingdom, was captured by the Dahomey. "European powers dictated trade terms with African kingdoms at that time," said Rico Chapman, history professor at Clark Atlanta University. "You help them enslave or you become enslaved. Many people couldn't resist the intrusion and those who didn't found themselves in the hulls of slave ships."

The Franco-Dahomean Wars were the beginning of the end of the Agojie's dominance and that of the Dahomey empire. When the region begrudgingly came under French rule, women were barred from the military and political and educational life. Some Agojie followed their king into exile in Martinique. The last surviving Agojie, Nawi, passed away at the age of 100 in 1979. The Agojie's "flaunting of ferocity, physical power and fearlessness was manipulated or corrupted as Europeans started to interpret [it] in their own context of what they felt societies should be," said Lynne Ellsworth Larson, in a *Smithsonian* article by Meilan Solly. Larson, an architectural historian, said that the Agojie upset the "understanding of gender roles and what women were supposed to do."

Journalists and historians Ana Lucia Araujo and Suzanne Preston Blier said that the Agojie descendants "remember their ancestors as brave

Portrait of Toussaint L'Ouverture.

was located, formally apologized for the nation's role in the slave trade. In 2002, Cyrille S. Oguin, Benin's ambassador to the US, toured America to speak to African descendants of the transatlantic slave trade, sharing his apologies, regrets, and hopes for reconciliation.

Oscar-winning actress Lupita Nyong'o, who also starred as Nakia, the Wakandan spy, in Marvel Studios' *Black Panther*, hosted a documentary called *Warrior Women with Lupita Nyong'o*, which followed the actress as she interviewed the current leader of the Dahomey and detailed the army's feats. The project was described as the uncovering of "a forgotten army." Moreover, the feature film *The Woman King*, starring Viola Davis and directed by Gina Prince-Bythewood, is a historical epic centered on the warrior women in the Kingdom of Dahomey.

women who fought as soldiers in an era of great violence for African women." In a story published in the *Washington Post*, they add that the Dahomey women were warriors "at a time when most Western white women were confined to domestic roles."

At the dawn of the twenty-first century, the officials in the nation of Benin, where the Dahomey Kingdom

The Dahomey warriors' resurgence upends falsehoods about women in history, their role in battle, and their leadership. Their infusion in the Dora Milaje tale gives Black Panther newfound resonance for contemporary women rethinking power.

In some ways, the dichotomy of power versus responsibility that Wakanda often wrestles with is an attempt to avoid the warmongering of the old Dahomey kingdom and the French colonial forces they partnered with who later overtook them. In *Intergalactic Empire*

An illustration of Dahomey warriors from the February 28, 1891, edition of *Le Petit Journal*.

of Wakanda, a robust Wakandan empire in space where enslavement is an accepted practice serves as a warning of this catastrophic parallel universe. Perhaps the Dora Milaje are a fictive reimagining of the Agojie, one where they and their leadership had a different vision of power. Although T'Challa is not a leader who enslaves, in *Intergalactic Empire of Wakanda*, as an enslaved person himself, he realizes that one's moral

Lupita Nyong'o as Nakia (left) and Letitia Wright as Shuri in a scene from *Black Panther* (2018), streaming now on Disney+.

Artwork from a variant cover of *Black Panther* #8, depicting Shuri, from November 2016.

fiber, in the throngs of power, can disintegrate.

The nature of power and how it is used is as much a subject for many of the non-royal women in Wakanda as it is for T'Challa. Nakia of *Intergalactic Empire of Wakanda*, who is a rebel to the villainous empire, leads the crew that rescues the enslaved T'Challa. Named after her Dora Milaje earthly predecessor, she channels the warrior legend of the Nakia of the past to overthrow the intergalactic empire and its enslaver regime. It is also intriguing that the challenges to the existence of a Wakandan monarchy on Earth largely come from women, many of whom are warriors, like Ayo and Aneka, or at least women who know the underbelly of war, like Zenzi. These women, unlike the vengeful Killmonger or self-serving Klaw are seeking to create a better community, a better nation. The risks are costly. Aneka, captain of the Dora Milaje, is sentenced to death (which Ayo rescues her from) for killing a chieftain who tormented girls when Wakanda was splintering. Moreover, a space-bound Nakia makes the ultimate sacrifice to dismantle the galactic empire.

Why is the warrior archetype so appealing? "The warrior goddess energy is about standing confidently in your power," said Lettie Sullivan, who provides

workshops on goddess culture. "It's the power of you that's always ready to take action to defend, to protect." Sullivan views the Dora Milaje as archetypes of their own. "It's a powerful archetypal energy to see a feminine warrior. There's something about the feminine when it takes all these shapes that is fascinating." In fact, she reasons that Shuri and Queen Ramonda are archetypes as well.

"Women, especially Western women, have been molded around this idea of being the damsel in distress, feeling like they aren't very capable or aren't strong. When you see someone like those of the Dora Milaje who hold the other polarity of that, someone who is brilliant, strong and then that coupled with the feminine, it's powerful."

The Dora Milaje appeal to women for an array of reasons. "I know a lot of women who came up without the protection of a man," said Sullivan, who also cosplays as Shuri. "In some ways the warrior archetype is where women had to pull energy from." In other cases, the Dora Milaje are exemplars of women standing in their truth and power. "To see a representation of that energy when it's called, respected, and exalted, that's where the magnetism lies," said Sullivan.

Art from the cover of *Shuri* #9, published June 2019.

COMPASSIONATE WARRIORS

Dr. Maya Green has been called a super hero for her work creating satellite testing centers and later vaccination centers in under-resourced areas during the Covid-19 pandemic. A Black Panther fan, she views the Dora Milaje as reminders of the women-led warrior spirit that protects families and neighborhoods. "I was actually very inspired by these women," said Green, who is regional medical director at Howard Brown Health in Chicago.

The Dora Milaje are more than mere warriors, they are also protectors and nurturers, much like the Wakandan deity, Bast. This multifaceted warrior is an idea that women relate to, said Green. "Whether we fight in the physical or the spiritual, financially, politically, we are soldiers on so many fronts," she said.

"If you go back and look at the beginning of the Covid-19 pandemic and who came out, you'll find a lot of women on the front lines. We were the soldiers," Green said. "We were doctors, nurses, elected officials, the people delivering food to people's doors. We were fighting COVID and nurturing the community to help people move

past this pandemic. We were the ones who put our lives at stake. The women of Wakanda embodied the nurturing, the strength, and the fearlessness.

"The women of Wakanda show that you don't have to be on the front lines. You can be in the lab creating things that protect your body and mind. When you fall, I will make potions, I will cook," she said. "Nurturing can be fighting. But you have to go beyond nurturing and lead."

Stephanie Evans, professor of Black women's studies at Georgia State University and a wellness advocate, admires the world of Wakanda for the spiritual balance that the Dora Milaje maintain. A longtime fan of the kung fu classic

36 Chambers, she compares the Dora Milaje to the fighting monks of Shaolin. "I'm interested in ethics and ethical self-defense," said Evans. "They're not mercenaries. They're not killers for hire. They are fighters for justice. That's why they are appealing to me."

This notion of conscious defenders is familiar to many girls.

"Women are the purveyors of safety in our homes and schools," said Kelly Fair. As CEO of Polished Pebbles Girls Mentoring Program, an organization with

ABOVE AND OPPOSITE: Shaolin monks.

Danai Gurira attends a screening of *Black Panther* (2018) at the Museum of Modern Art in New York on February 13, 2018.

some 400 mentors, Fair notes that girls in her mentoring program developed new respect for their moms during the pandemic, often watching them bring their office work home or realizing that their mothers were first responders. "I think that the way Black women take care of the community is similar to the way they do in Wakanda."

Moreover, the stylings of the women themselves reorders femininity. Many of the Dora Milaje are bald, a familiar style among Black women, but often one that's deemed unfeminine in Western spaces. With some Black women undergoing the big chop, a major haircut to allow them to either "go natural" or wear as a style itself, the regal elegance of the Dora Milaje was uplifting.

"They show the power in the bald head," said Evans, who herself had the big chop. "I am not my hair," she adds, quoting an India.Arie song. Evans views bald style as a rite of passage, an evolution into maturity, and a reclaiming of beauty. The style, one first noted in Hudlin's writings, allows some of the Dora Milaje to stand boldly in their power.

"Okoye flies in the face of our conventional ideas of femininity, while still functioning within her own definition of feminist," said Danai Gurira, who played Okoye in the film. "She doesn't take to the conventions of how the rest of world says a woman should wear her hair, for instance. But she also always has a big red lip on, a lot of lash—without ever compromising her philosophy. She lives contentedly within both."

There's strength in femininity, though the celebration of being a "strong woman" doesn't always address the nuanced expectations women face, like taking on too many responsibilities and feeling like they can't ask for help. Fair sometimes works with girls who readily admit that they have anger issues but aren't sure how to reconcile with the emotion, holding in their emotions and wrestling to control them. Fair hopes more can be gleaned from Panther lore about how young girls can deal with trauma. "I think there's opportunity in thinking on how did these women deal with tragedy? How do they deal with aggression and anger?" she says, noting that girls crave healthy ways to deal with anger management. "There are some deeper lessons here."

Perhaps there are some that can be found in the stories of the rebel Nigandan leader and Black Panther nemesis, Zenzi. Zenzi mastered the ability to bring her enemies' volatile emotions to the surface to use against them and seeks to "return Wakanda" to the people. In *The Intergalactic Empire of Wakanda*, Zenzi finds herself looking to Bast for guidance. She ultimately merges with the childlike Bast, which helps Bast restore her powers and dissolves Zenzi's vengeance, rolling the young leader's identity into Bast's own. Zenzi's anger is transmuted into power.

Zenzi on the cover of *Black Panther* #11, published April 24, 2019.

Black Panther's helmet at the Marvel's Avengers S.T.A.T.I.O.N. at ExCeL in London in 2018.

IN THE LAB

When digital artist Nettrice Gaskins was talking about design, Afrofuturism, and science to a group of African American and Latinx kids in Boston some years back, she used Shuri as her shining example. She explained how Shuri was the lead designer in Wakanda, making wearable technology, including the Panther's suit. Then she showed them a self-made Dora Milaje boot that lit up, and the kids swarmed her. They wanted to know how to make the boot. How could *they* redesign a world? "One girl came up to me and said she wanted to be the Shuri of healthcare," Gaskins remembered.

Gaskins is most known for her groundbreaking art created with artificial intelligence. Her rendition of culture critic Greg Tate was a public artwork in Brooklyn and her profiles of Black scientists were displayed in the National Museum of African American History and Culture. However, Gaskins also works with organizations to create maker labs and curricula for kids of color. She cocreated a Black Panther–inspired curriculum for Fab Lab on bringing digital fabrication into the classroom.

"Many kids struggled to name an innovator, engineer, or inventor in their life," says Gaskins, whose mother was a mathematician. Shuri is a connection. "Shuri is an engineer, she's a maker.

Costumes worn by *Black Panther* (2018) characters, from left, Okoye, Black Panther, and Shuri, on display in 2018 during a preview of the exhibit Marvel: Universe of Super Heroes at the Museum of Pop Culture in Seattle, Washington.

Ruth Carter, winner of Best Costume Design for *Black Panther* (2018), at the 91st Annual Academy Awards.

She prototypes, she designs. She has a lab and people work with her." For the students, the light-up Dora Milaje boot made engineering more tangible.

When Gaskins was a teen, she was part of one of the early maker labs, a space where teens could tinker with electronics and make prototypes. "It was the late '80s. I said in ten years, design labs in schools and community-based maker labs will be everywhere. Ten years out, twenty years out, thirty years out, we're still not there."

"In my current job we visit youth centers and help them build things they didn't imagine they could build, with that same idea of tinkering, the same spirit of Shuri," said Gaskins, who works with the Lesley University STEAM Learning Lab. Youth-centered labs could even be named after characters in Wakanda. Whether one calls it the Shuri Lab or Wakanda, says Gaskins, what's most important is that such spaces have electronics, 3D printing, laser cutters, and other equipment where students can imagine, prototype, and experiment. Living the Shuri life is a question of access and equity. However, it also poses the question of who is allowed to innovate. "Students pick up on subconscious messages about who scientists are and what they look like," said Gaskins, from media and perhaps even from biases in their schools.

Gaskins says that the embedding of culture in the technology, an idea also pushed by costume designer Ruth Carter and production designer Hannah Beachler in *Black Panther*, is one that she hopes to duplicate with students. Her book, *Techno-Vernacular Creativity and Innovation: Culturally Relevant Making Inside and Outside of the Classroom*, is a guide for teachers looking to adopt STEAM in education programs.

Currently, she's working with an African American math teacher in New Jersey and helping him use the legendary Gee's Bend quilts to teach math to mostly African American and Latinx students. The quilts are a part of a century-plus-old African American quilting tradition from Alabama. Students are engaged, studying patterns and asking questions. "Next week they'll make a quilt using math," she said. The grant-funded program is generating interest. "We're prototyping how to take this framework and move it into math or electronics or design like Shuri," she says. Black Panther normalizes women in leadership and science. The impact of their presence, much like the *Star Trek* character Uhura, will unfold in unprecedented ways.

Hannah Beachler poses in the press room during the 2019 Academy Awards, after winning Best Production Design for *Black Panther* (2018).

PEOPLE POWER

"Madam, despite being royalty, T'Challa has always put the good of the people first. Any investigation will determine nothing less."
—Akili, *The Long Shadow*, Book 5

CHAPTER 5

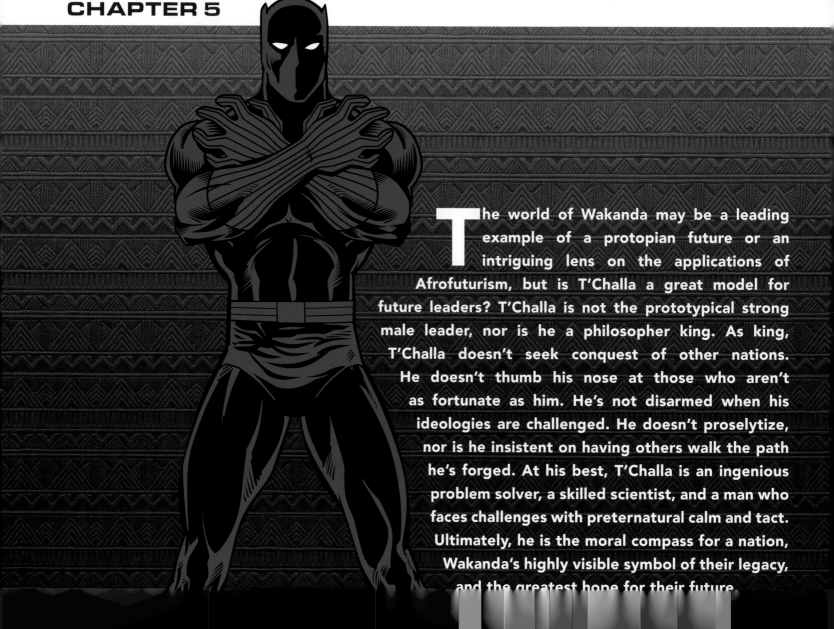

The world of Wakanda may be a leading example of a protopian future or an intriguing lens on the applications of Afrofuturism, but is T'Challa a great model for future leaders? T'Challa is not the prototypical strong male leader, nor is he a philosopher king. As king, T'Challa doesn't seek conquest of other nations. He doesn't thumb his nose at those who aren't as fortunate as him. He's not disarmed when his ideologies are challenged. He doesn't proselytize, nor is he insistent on having others walk the path he's forged. At his best, T'Challa is an ingenious problem solver, a skilled scientist, and a man who faces challenges with preternatural calm and tact. Ultimately, he is the moral compass for a nation, Wakanda's highly visible symbol of their legacy, and the greatest hope for their future.

T'Challa has tenacity, says culture critic Miles Marshall Lewis: "T'Challa's tenacity reminds me of the same 'ass power' that Quincy Jones has always talked about—the ability to keep your behind in the chair until the task is complete. Whether as the King of Wakanda or as an Afrofuturist super hero battling the likes of Killmonger or the KKK, Black Panther never gives up." There's a lesson in this stick-to-itiveness for future leaders. "Through whatever means necessary (meditation, exercise, nourishing mental health), the ability to wake up fresh daily to chip away at life's goals and challenges is an invaluable leadership trait."

Both problem solver and visionary, T'Challa never loses sight of the goal: to defend and protect Wakanda. But how he defends and protects Wakanda is subject to change.

Much of *A Nation Under Our Feet*, *The Intergalactic Empire of Wakanda*, and *The Long Shadow* explores a Wakanda evolving from monarchy to a parliamentary democracy. The transformation isn't easy. The nation, at times, seems on the verge of splintering. But Wakanda's issues aren't resolved by T'Challa's death-defying feats or his intellect alone. As a collective, the people of Wakanda realize they are all responsible for the Wakandan future and claim an active governing role in ruling the nation. T'Challa's shifting role from hereditary monarch

Cover art for the first issue of Ta-Nehisi Coates' *Black Panther*, published April 2016.

Martin Luther King Jr. in 1964.

capacity for change prepares him for a new, uncertain future.

"They've lost their faith in me, and they show it. But faith is earned. Even as I run, even as I fight, I know I have some things to prove and trust to win back."

—T'Challa, *The Long Shadow*, Book 5

Afrofuturist NFT world creator, Kwame Michael-Nana Brako, known as DarkMythst, most admires T'Challa's comfort with uncharted treks. The leader's foray into ceremonial leader may be his greatest challenge yet. "There's a sense of being comfortable with the unknown," says DarkMythst. "He knows there's no such thing as failure and that it's all about lessons learned." Leadership coach Monique Spence says that T'Challa is a good example of someone who has an appreciation for insights from the ancestors. "He didn't have to repeat the mistakes of the past," she said.

MAN OF MANY LIVES

T'Challa is the leader with ten crowns on his head. At one point, he was ruling monarch of Wakanda, Emperor of Wakanda's interstellar sister empire, chairman of the Avengers, and reigning Black Panther all at once. Christopher Priest is credited with bringing the cool factor to T'Challa, but T'Challa may be the one who brings a sense of ease to juggling his dilemmas. "He doesn't break a sweat," said Terry Gant, owner of Third Coast Comics. Unlike his

to ceremonial king still requires that he be a leader in the new democracy. His commitment to Wakandan ideals may be among his strongest qualities. However, his

peers in the Avengers, T'Challa is responsible to a nation, thus his temperament feels more mature than that of his cohorts. His ability to multitask is ranked among the gods. He can keep the Wakandan economy afloat while fighting the likes of Mephisto or snatch the reins of a distorted interstellar Wakanda while struggling to get back to a divided nation bent on undoing the monarchy.

"I grew up in the '70s on my father's leftover comic books and I remember Black Panther defeating the entire Fantastic Four in his very first appearance from 1966," said Lewis. "Reed Richards, the FF's leader, was always

Black Panther in *Ultimates* #8, published June 2016.

nth-degree level genius, and it wasn't even a superpower. The fact that T'Challa devised a way to beat them all proved his intelligence to me." With his intelligence comes discernment. T'Challa is able to sort out truths from nontruths. "The intelligence to detect propaganda will become increasingly valuable in order to lead."

"Change does not roll in on the wheels of inevitability, but comes through continuous struggle."

—Martin Luther King Jr.

A mural of Martin Luther King Jr. inside Graffiti Alley in Boston, Massachusetts.

T'Challa has fairly high ideals and is quite grounded for a king. Though T'Challa is not an advocate of nonviolence, his approach to leadership resonates with another man named King. "The ultimate measure of a man is not where he stands in moments of convenience and comfort, but where he stands at times of challenge and controversy," Martin Luther King Jr. once said. King, too, put the welfare of those he advocated for before all else, a trait to which T'Challa easily relates. When King said, "I submit to you that if a man has not discovered something that he will die for, he isn't fit to live," he sounds like T'Challa. More than anything, T'Challa is similar to the civil rights icon because they share compassion and conviction.

As a communicator, T'Challa listens more than he speaks. Traci Evans, owner of the boutique Meow and Barks, is a strong supporter of women in leadership. Women in business often battle with men who have tough times working with women in leadership. A Black Panther fan, she admires the image of T'Challa, a respected king, working and surrounding himself with talented women in power. "One feels understood in his presence," says Evans, who so closely identifies with the women characters in Wakanda that T'Challa's trust in their talents feels like a trust in her own. Evans is in awe of the Black Panther's respect for women in leadership, a trait she hopes more men will adopt. "He respects everyone's intellect," says Evans. "He knows how to let women be their best selves and defend."

As duty requires, T'Challa always puts the betterment of his nation before all else. Yet he doesn't seek accolades. As the leader of an uncolonized nation, T'Challa's not interested in conquest. "Conquest isn't important to him," says futurist Monika Bielskyte. "Conquest has nothing to do with the well-being of your citizens or the development

David Flores' "World Stage Legacy" mural along the back entrance of the Los Angeles Memorial Coliseum, featuring Martin Luther King Jr. (right) and John F. Kennedy.

Portrait of Kwame Nkrumah, the first prime minister and later first president of Ghana.

of people." He's committed to the safety and well-being of Wakandans along with the general well-being of humanity at large.

T'Challa rarely says no when presented with the opportunity to lead. He's a natural leader, one who rules with grace and considers all sides. "Some people who are good at leading are always put in situations where they have to lead," said DarkMythst. "People look to them to do so, regardless of whether they want to or not." Moreover, T'Challa seems to genuinely care about the people he's responsible for. He's very no-nonsense but he is gracious. "There's a sense of empathy, sympathy, and equality that he has that's necessary for the future," said DarkMythst.

T'Challa isn't afraid to stand up for what's right. In fact, he doesn't appear to be afraid of anything. Although he confides his concerns to his best friend, Storm; his stepmother, Queen Ramonda; and his sister, Shuri, he transmutes worry into action. With his ancestors behind him and a nation or sometimes a world depending on him, T'Challa doesn't capitulate to his fears. He's made a habit of transcending them.

"**Without dignity there is no liberty, without justice there is no dignity, and without independence there are no free men.**"

—Patrice Lumumba, in a letter from
Thysville Prison, *Congo, My Country*

"People think of T'Challa as a pan-African leader or a social justice leader, but he's really leader of Wakanda," said John Jennings, a graphic novelist and comics scholar. Like many adept leaders on the national scene, T'Challa's symbolism and work takes him beyond Wakanda-specific issues. Fighting vampires in New Orleans in the aftermath of Hurricane Katrina or the KKK at any time is not a Wakandan affair. Yet, T'Challa's humanity doesn't limit him to resolving problems at home alone, a departure from his isolationist predecessors, who even in their spirit form encourage putting all things Wakanda first. The stark differences between his patient, albeit conventional, father, T'Chaka, and T'Challa frustrates the changing king.

"**I have done everything that could be expected of me—sacrificed everything for my people, everything for my nation. My own desires, my own marriage. I have committed murder, many, many times. I have done all of this for Wakanda—with head held high, and no regard for self. How dare you doubt me, Father?**"

—T'Challa (*A Nation Under Our Feet*)

There's a fascination with T'Challa's style and balance. "He's a young leader and young leaders have vigor," said Ajani Brown, professor of Africana Studies at San Diego State University. "His zeal to protect his people is astounding." The Wakandan leader is forever wedged

between the isolationist desires of his forefathers and the quest to have Wakanda influence the world. He is always leagues ahead of his opponents, crafting plans faster than readers can catch up with them. "He's a blend of Ghanian president Kwame Nkrumah and South African President Nelson Mandela," says Brown. Noting the romanticized youth of John F. Kennedy and the youth leadership of the Black Panther Party, Brown says that T'Challa, too, will always be locked in time. "He is a perpetual young leader."

Kwame Nkrumah, standing on stool, at his inauguration as the first president of the Republic of Ghana in 1960.

Nelson Mandela speaking at a meeting in South Africa in October 1990.

EARNING THE MANTLE OF LEADER

Leadership experts have found wisdom in the elegant world of Wakandan politics. From the comic pages to the film itself, Black Panther isn't short of power struggles. Colonel Cherie Roff took to the *Joint Base Charleston*, a military publication, to share the leadership models in Wakanda. "The movie represented the status-quo leader example in the main character T'Challa/Black Panther. The change agent or courageous leader example is the love interest Nakia. The integrity dilemma leader is the commanding General Okoye, and the toxic leader is the villain Erik Killmonger," she writes. She encouraged readers to "look at the leadership displayed by the characters and determine your path to that inspirational and courageous leader."

Business writer LaSonya Berry penned an essay on leadership traits in the *Diversity Professional* and praised the Black Panther mythos for celebrating a title earned. Although T'Challa's title as king was hereditary, his duty as Black Panther was hard-earned. The process of becoming Black Panther isn't easy, and that tough path was appealing to the Wakandan people, who require that their leaders be doused in Bast's prowess. "Organizations that assign leadership roles because of any reason other than earning it create a culture of low expectations, conflict, and disengagement," said Berry. She also lists loyalty and transparency as desirable leadership traits that T'Challa extols.

Obligatory loyalty from Wakandans would ultimately come into question in the comics. For much of T'Challa's leadership, the allegiance of the Dora Milaje and his family, with the notable exception of his stepbrother, White Wolf, went unquestioned. Killmonger was the first to challenge T'Challa's rights to lead. White Wolf failed in his attempts to get T'Challa to compromise his morals as Wakandan protector. Rebel factions would question T'Challa's commitment to all the ethnic groups of Wakanda. T'Challa's efforts to quell internal dissent became increasingly complicated.

"Good leaders can only exist in the context where there is a strong basis of citizenship," said Bristol-based Afrofuturist playwright and historian Edson Burton. "You don't develop one level of stakeholders and not others. Society must be working towards a state of cohesion."

The King of the Xhosa people, King Xolilizwe Sigcawu, awarded Nelson Mandela (pictured) the ancient tribal warrior honor of the Isithwalandwe Sesizwe, in South Africa.

Cover art for *Black Panther* #15, published August 2019.

LIMITS OF A KING

T'Challa grew into a thoughtful, intelligent leader, but also an authoritarian one. He was magnanimous, but he was also king. On the one hand, T'Challa appears to be fairly collaborative. He's a team player with the Avengers and the Crew, and is often called upon to lead. He works with Shuri, consults Quewen Ramonda, and works collaboratively with the Dora Milaje. However, he has a tendency to keep the decision-making process to himself, keeping his cards close to the vest. His lack of trust is legitimate. The latest leader in an old lineage, he has both a nation on Earth and one in space to defend, not to mention a world to save.

But this reluctance to share his plans and struggles, paired with a waning lack of transparency and his periodic, sometimes unexplained absences from Wakanda (teaching in Harlem, fighting with the Avengers, taking part in covert missions against the Wakandan secret police) eventually sparked warring factions and a demand for democracy. His trust has limits, and the secrecy that is often acceptable in the role of a monarch is not a privilege he's eager to give up as his role evolves.

Playwright Burton takes issue with the celebration of the king in the reclamation of Black identities. Monarchy rule as absolute power or divine rule leaves a populace unempowered. The class implications, one in which the royals can live a life of abundance that the rest of the population can never hope to reach, is problematic, Burton says. Hereditary rule undermines a population's self-determination and can keep them hostage to the whims of leadership. However, Burton is delighted with T'Challa's role as ceremonial king, rather than absolute monarch, and believes it's a better way to inspire future models of leadership.

"We've been brought up hearing the stories of European kings and queens and then we want to hear our stories about kings and queens. It's good to hear stories and learn from them," he said. "But when it comes to the best forms of governance for humans, monarchies aren't good for anyone." The romanticizing of the role of king as the ultimate in dignity and power is one of fantasy. "When I hear people say they came from kings and queens, I say I'm happy to descend from a peasant. Everyone has an innate dignity and spirit. It's that dignity that needs to be nurtured and kindled."

Jordan Ifueko, author of *Raybearer* and its sequel, *Redemptor*, found herself contemplating these same ideas in constructing her story. Tarisai, the protagonist, joins a collective of children raised in a royal court to advise the prince in training. Tarisai comes into her own power and regal bearing, but questions of what to do with her power are central to her rise.

"There is a line in *Redemptor* where she talks about how maybe the only true virtuous use of power is to find

Cover art for *Black Panther* #18, published November 2019.

a way to share it with others," Ifueko said in a virtual book talk for Charis Circle, the nonprofit programming arm of Charis Books in Decatur, Georgia.

Detail from the cover art of *Ironheart* #9, which finds main character Riri Williams (center right) in Wakanda.

"It was a hard balance to strike. On one hand, Black girls in particular need the story of being revered by their community and lifted up. [Tarisai] is thought of almost as a goddess by the majority of this massive empire which I think is the kind of representation that Black girls need. But we can't stop there. We have to look at should empires even exist. When representation means perpetuating a power structure that will ultimately keep down those who need representation most, that's something we have to think about more in our fantasy, sci-fi, and Afrofuturism."

As the power structure in Wakanda changes, T'Challa's role is his country transitions too. Some of these changes reflect the beliefs of writers who, in acknowledging Wakanda's proximity to utopia, wanted to rework power structures. With the dawning of a new democracy and a diminished royal stature, T'Challa must engage his new council in his works as Black Panther. T'Challa can no longer launch missions without first seeking approval. This shift from absolute power to ceremonial king is not an easy one for T'Challa. His hesitancy to share the existence of the Wakandan sleeper agents, the secret Wakandan empire beyond the galaxy, or his covert mission to find the assassin targeting his agents becomes the arc for "The Long Shadow." The country, which prides itself on never being colonized, doesn't want to be beholden in a new era of compromises, either. T'Challa is arrested for his transgressions and breaks out to regain the trust of his people and uncover the entities trying to undermine the new democracy.

Regardless of T'Challa's wrestling with change, he's largely respected as one who strives to make the right decision. "The time is always right to do what is

Artwork from a variant cover of *Black Panther: World of Wakanda* #2, featuring Dora Milaje Ayo and Aneka.

Dora Milaje Aneka and Ayo in a variant cover by Esad Ribic for *Black Panther* #7, published October 2016.

right," Martin Luther King Jr. once said. T'Challa's childhood tragedy of losing his father and becoming king was eased somewhat by the guiding wisdom of the ancestors. Did T'Challa become king too soon? Are his global escapades in part a desire to explore life beyond the monarchy? "He's the king who doesn't want to be king who keeps getting asked to lead," says John Jennings. Perhaps being king and leading is all T'Challa knows. Being good at it just seems to attract more responsibility. While fans debate T'Challa's motivations, they largely agree that T'Challa is one of the best leaders in the Marvel Universe.

It came as a bit of a surprise when T'Challa stepped down as chairman of the Avengers in *Avengers* #55 (2022). Even Captain America had once wondered whether the Wakandan leader was stretching himself too thin. But fans didn't lose faith in T'Challa's leadership ability.

"T'Challa is by no means a poor leader. To lead the Avengers would require the utmost devotion to the team and the betterment of the world, and as a king, T'Challa could never put the Avengers before Wakanda in his mind," writes Nicholas Brooks at *CBR.com*. "As a result, he shouldered everything and proved that he still had many secrets. This is something which a leader should never have among their peers if it could be used against them. That said, if there were ever a time when he could devote his attention to the Avengers wholeheartedly, he would be one of the best leaders in the team's storied history."

"Everyone wins when knowledge is shared," writes business pundit Omar L. Harris. He lists the quip as one of six business lessons gleaned from Black Panther. Wakanda's isolationist and protectionist history, while understandable, may have trickled into T'Challa's leadership in ways that belie his desire for the nation to be influential on the world stage. He has a spiritual obligation to the nation to ensure that it is always exceptional and willing to question itself.

T'Challa understood his personal power and the power in his role, said Monique Spence, a Black Panther fan and leadership coach. Spence often works with clients to help them tap into their personal power. "He had a knowing. Some of us have a hoping," said Spence of T'Challa. "To see people having a knowing of their power and their worth is a very valuable reflection and one of my greatest takeaways from his story."

How should a leader in a postcolonial nation lead? Perhaps that style is one to be determined by the people who hold him accountable.

"A good leader should wish to be replaced," said Burton. "Maybe a good god creates people who one day don't need them."

Artwork from the cover of *Black Panther* #2, published May 2016.

PORTAL PRESENCE

CHAPTER 6

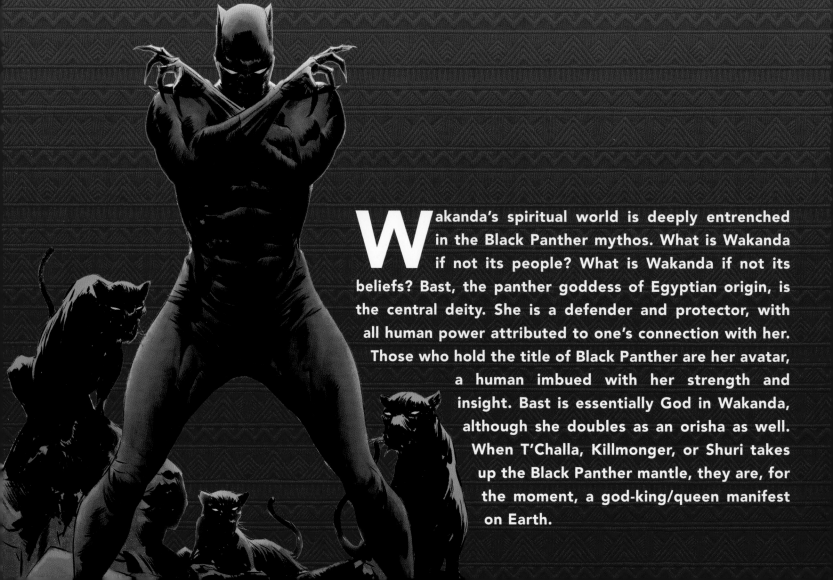

Wakanda's spiritual world is deeply entrenched in the Black Panther mythos. What is Wakanda if not its people? What is Wakanda if not its beliefs? Bast, the panther goddess of Egyptian origin, is the central deity. She is a defender and protector, with all human power attributed to one's connection with her. Those who hold the title of Black Panther are her avatar, a human imbued with her strength and insight. Bast is essentially God in Wakanda, although she doubles as an orisha as well. When T'Challa, Killmonger, or Shuri takes up the Black Panther mantle, they are, for the moment, a god-king/queen manifest on Earth.

The orishas, a team of spirits, stand as principled protectors. Moreover, Djalia, the plane of Wakandan memory, is an akashic records of ancestral knowledge.

The Wakandan faith is a synthesis of pantheons in African cultures, remixing many deities that are honored today. Pulling from familiar beliefs originating in Ancient Egypt, the Yoruba, and the Lovedu, among others, the Wakandan spiritual realm spans the African continent and Diaspora. These harbingers of belief enrich the story. Renowned writer, healer, and Dagara elder Malidoma Patrice Somé of the West African nation of Burkina Faso writes about symbols in his book, *The Healing Wisdom of Africa: Finding Life Purpose Through Nature, Ritual, and Community.* "Symbols are the doorway to ritual," he says. Just as our bodies can't survive without nourishment, our psyches cannot sustain themselves without symbolism."

This synthesis of spirits is a familiar practice. Remixing is an Afrofuturist aesthetic, and the syncretizing of beliefs in the creation of the Wakandan faith is no different. The integration of such deities is part reclamation, part Afrofuturist practice. There are many African Diasporic practices, from hoodoo to New Orleans voodoo, that have a blend of sources. La Regla de Ocha in parts of Latin America, including Cuba and Puerto Rico, and Candomblé in Brazil are syncretizations of Ifa, a religion of the Yoruba in Nigeria, Benin, and Togo, with Christianity. The two were sometimes blended in part to hide the practice of African religions during periods where they were outlawed. Early African American places of worship during enslavement often had Islamic symbols carved in the benches. Many Muslims in West Africa also

acknowledge African indigenous spirits. Hoodoo is a blend of spirituality from the Congo region, European, and indigenous practices. Some voodoo practitioners today integrate the orishas.

Shuri as the Black Panther on the cover of *Black Panther* #4 from May 2009.

"It almost comes natural from our historical experience," said Rico Wade, director of Digital Humanities at Clark Atlanta University. "With the Transatlantic slave trade, plantation societies, all these African spiritualities, and storytelling as a technology, centuries later, it's natural that we blend without even thinking about it."

But the synthesis of spiritual practices during enslavement and the aftermath were not happenstance. "I think people think that that were syncretized were done so by circumstance. These things didn't happen to come together, but were brought together because they had similarities," said Kinitra Brooks, an Ifa practitioner and endowed chair in literary studies at Michigan State University. "They understood the metaphysics of what they were bringing together. These people were studied in what they were bringing together and some were long-term priests. There's nothing happenstance about this."

The creation of hybrid pantheons and histories in Afrofuturist or Black speculative stories is technology itself. "Story is the first technology," said John Jennings, who adapted Octavia Butler's *Kindred* and *Parable of the Sower* into graphic novels. "Myths are how we make sense of the world."

The streams of thought in Afrofuturist or Black Speculative stories also assert a way of thinking about society. Author Saidiya Hartman calls this practice fabulation, a combination of historical and archival research with critical theory and fictional narrative to fill in the blanks left in the historical record. However, humans are always seeking to know themselves. "I don't know if we can write a Black speculative story without a spiritual practice or some way that people make sense of their world," said Jennings.

It's essential for world-building but it's also foundational for creating worlds informed by wisdom from Black cultures. The main character in Butler's *Parable of the Sower* documented fragments of wisdom in her journal as a book to help people move out of a dystopian world. Samuel Delaney's *Nova* uses the tarot and astronomy as the interplanetary practice. "God or these spiritual beliefs are another way for people to understand how energy works," says Tim Fielder, a fan of *Nova* who also created art based on Delaney's novel that was featured at Carnegie Hall's Afrofuturism Festival.

Haitian American author Fabrice Guerrier includes Vodun in his writing. "The story wouldn't be the story without spirituality," he said of his works. "For me, these gods or mythological structures, whether one believes or not, are a way for us to bring to life aspects of emotion," said Guerrier. Guerrier founded the international sci-fi writing collective Syllble and appreciates storytelling that uses cosmology and myth as a window to soul-enriching experiences. "I'm trying to find things that are truthful that make the story timeless," he said.

Brooks says that many Black creators are looking for African ways of understanding the world that have a propensity for blending. "People are making their own spiritual journeys and they find Black spiritual pantheons speaking to those explorations." However, as a practitioner, she notes that all African religious practices can't be merged. "You don't practice vodun and call them orisha because you're dealing with Fon and Dahomey energies, which are different from Yoruba energies. To mix them together is not just disrespectful but dangerous."

Black Panther writer Ta-Nehisi Coates added several spiritual dimensions to the Wakandan world. Though he himself is an atheist, he says the evolution of Storm into a Wakandan orisha, a story arc he crafted, and her worship made sense to him. In an interview with fellow Black Panther writer Evan Narcisse, Narcisse asked how the acclaimed author could incorporate devotion when spirituality isn't a part of his practice.

"Because I understand it. I get it," Coates said in an interview with Evan Narcisse for *Polygon.com* in 2021. "It's in our brains, the reflex to order the world. It's hard even for me to think about the awesomeness of the universe and think of it just as pure chaos, with no purpose or guidance. It kind of breaks something about the human brain. So, I very much get the need and the understanding. That doesn't feel so foreign to me."

PANTHER JOURNEY

With Bast as the overarching deity in Wakanda, Ancient Egyptian beliefs were always embedded in the Black Panther story. However, the crossing of pantheon lore first began in the late '90s. In *Black Panther* #21, T'Challa's Ka (an Egyptian word for spirit), in consort with the hero Moon Knight, are in an ancestral realm of Black Panthers dubbed both the Panther Pavilion and the Land of the Dead. Brother Voodoo, a hero charged with the powers of the Vodun loa, or high-powered ancestors, tries to keep T'Challa alive. T'Challa is too weak to connect with Bast, so Brother Voodoo uses his trance state to create a gateway where Moon Knight and T'Challa can gain power from another Egyptian deity, Khonsu. Khonsu, a moon god, is the guardian power of Moon Knight and also a healer. Black Panther and Moon Knight must then defeat the Ennead, Ancient Egypt's league of gods and goddesses, to resurrect a slaughtered ancestor whose ka are destroyed, only to discover that Nightmare is feeding on them.

Black Panther and Moon Knight find the famous Egyptian *Book of the Dead*, a manual for the afterlife, which T'Challa says is filled with healing secrets. Book in hand, they enter Khonsu's sarcophagus and are charged by the god to go on a pilgrimage to commune with Bast. But that pilgrimage is a battle with Nightmare, who claims that to destroy the *Book of the Dead* will destroy them all. But Black Panther outwits Nightmare and defeats him by destroying the ancient text, an act that brings T'Challa back to life, restores the Panther ancestors, and traps Nightmare in a world of his own making.

This is, essentially, a shamanistic journey, a lesson-fueled out-of-body experience. Black Panther is, in a sense, reborn. Not to mention that this happens amid Killmonger being brought back to life in the Resurrection Altar, a nod to both Christianity and vodun. The story, written by Christopher Priest, inverted the roles of the Ennead, who typically serve as inspired guides for humans and are a mix of male and female deities. Here, they are mostly male protectors of Khonsu. The story reestablished Wakanda in a broader Egyptian realm of gods. If T'Challa is the avatar of one Egyptian god, it would only make sense that he could access the insight of another.

T'Challa has often found himself in altered realms. The young king was caught between worlds, on the plane between life and death, in the series *Shuri*, written by Reginald Hudlin. Zawavari, a near-immortal shaman, ushered both Storm and Shuri into the realm utilizing their mind power, so they could rescue T'Challa. T'Challa battled the vampire Morlun and a legion of undead. However, the escapade became a moment to uplift the value of shamans and spiritual gifts in Wakanda's technotopia. Fresh from Bast's rejection of her bid to be Black Panther, Shuri realizes she didn't know the ways of spirit. She, too, embarks on the task to go into the in-between world to reclaim her relationship with the spirit world and save her brother. "My pride was my defeat," she learns. "I trusted too much in the scientific training I'd been given. I trusted too much in fighting skills and tactics, in my fight to become Wakanda's weapon in her hour of need." Entering the realm and defeating the foe was part of the rite of passage.

Representing a West African goddess, a float in the Oshun Carnival parade cruises down St. Charles Avenue in New Orleans in February 2007.

ORISHAS REIMAGINED

Pop stars from Beyoncé to Princess Nokia have invoked orishas in their work. Ta-Nehisi Coates added the orishas to the Panther lore. Comprised of Thoth, Ptah, Mujaji, Kokou, and Nyame, they serve as both energy centers and wisdom council. Typically, the term *orisha* refers to the Ifa spirits, a realm of earthly entities who can number in the hundreds. Symbolized by male and female spirits alike, these spirits oversee aspects of life and nature, with Ochun and Shango being among the most revered. Ifa is the most practiced African religion in the Americas, typically practiced as the African-derived religions Santeria and Candomble, with a smaller pantheon.

There's a belief that the orishas were at one point people themselves. "The power of the orishas is not an intangible, mystical force nurtured by the faith of the believers," said Migene González-Wippler, a cultural anthropologist, in her book *Santería: The Religion*. "It is not something sublimely ethereal that sustains the soul and gives it strength through faith. It is raw energy, awesome power visually and materially discernable." The orishas provide protection and help in times of need, she says.

In Wakanda, these orishas comprise a mix of African spiritual worlds. Rather than create fictitious deities to

inspire Wakandans, Coates pulled from existing beliefs. After all, two creator gods, a scribe, two rain goddesses, and a warrior spirit make for a unique council of spirits. These orishas, sometimes also called orishas and loa, largely remain mysterious to T'Challa, standing as a presence when he's made an emotional evolution or a waiting presence during a transmutation or the rebirth of a god. Bast, who in the story calls herself an orisha as well, is the only one who engages with him directly.

Two of the Wakanda orishas, Ptah and Thoth, originated in Lower Egypt. Ptah is the creator in the Ancient Egyptian world. He created himself and all who came afterward. Revered by craftsmen and architects, he was prominent during all the antiquity periods in Ancient Egypt and much of North Africa. Ptah was the favored deity of the legendary

LEFT: Pedestal for a Shango shrine, early twentieth century. RIGHT: Dance wand for a Shango devotee.

Art of Thoth.

Imhotep, the Egyptian vizier and architect of pyramids. "He willed the world into existence with the power of his mind, like a great conjuror of celestial proportions," said Kristopher Henke in *The Collector*. "Not satisfied there, he uses his speech to give life to his creation."

Thoth is actually the Ancient Egyptian deity for scribes and writers, said to have invented writing and created language. Thoth is usually visualized with the head of the sacred ibis. The great interpreter for the sun god Ra, he is married to Maat, the deity of justice and balance. The *Book of the Dead* and other ancient texts are accredited to Thoth and a rumored book in his name allegedly contains the secrets of the universe.

The name of another Wakandan orisha, Nyame, is the Twi word for God. Twi is an Akan language spoken in Ghana. Appearing as both male and female, Nyame is acknowledged by the Akan and the Ashanti of Ghana. Kokou, or Flimani Koku, is both a warrior loa in vodun in Benin and Togo as well as an orisha in Nigeria today. He serves as a protector and is celebrated at an annual festival in Benin. Mujaji is a rain goddess with South African origins. The honorary title given to queens of the Lovedu, Mujaji can control the clouds and sway the rains with her emotions. She is the bringer of sustenance and can punish with drought.

Storm is the only orisha who didn't come from a real-world pantheon. A favorite among the X-Men and T'Challa's best friend and former wife, she was inspired by existing rain goddesses like Mujaji. Storm's rise to orisha honors her contributions to Wakanda and parallels stories of the orisha's human origin. In fact, Storm believes she has supplanted her fellow orishas. When the orisha appear after a long absence to support T'Challa in his battle against the Emperor of Wakanda's realm in distance galaxies, all are surprised. "Well, there's not exactly a God Network," says Storm in *Black Panther* #23 (2018). "And technically I replaced the orisha as much as I joined them."

Coates made other adjustments to the Wakandan world, adding oracles as consultants to Wakandans in need. Coates also formalized the Panther Pavilion as Djalia, the Plane of Wakandan Memory. The realm may be named after the Dja River, which borders the Republic of the Congo and Cameroon. The film *Black Panther* also incorporated Djalia, referring to it as the Ancestral Plain. T'Challa was sent to the realm, with the help of shaman and the Heart-Shaped Herb, to speak to his father and later to confront his ancestors for failing to aid those in need across the world.

The Wakandan spiritual world pulls from enough pantheons that anyone with a relationship to African religions can see a familiar symbol. For anyone questioning the role of God or spirits in their lives, there's an existential quest embedded in the Black Panther's story too.

A statue of Thoth.

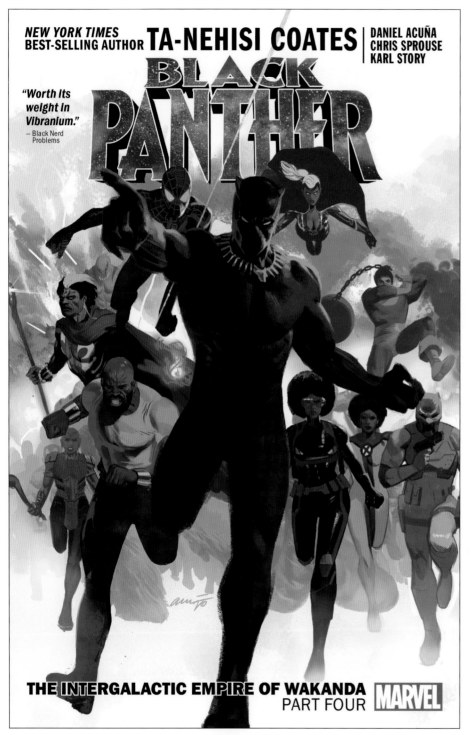

NEW YORK TIMES BEST-SELLING AUTHOR **TA-NEHISI COATES** | DANIEL ACUÑA CHRIS SPROUSE KARL STORY

BLACK PANTHER

"Worth its weight in Vibranium."
— Black Nerd Problems

THE INTERGALACTIC EMPIRE OF WAKANDA PART FOUR **MARVEL**

Cover of *Black Panther Book 9: The Intergalactic Empire of Wakanda Part Four*, which collects Black Panther #19–25, written by Ta-Nehisi Coates. This trade paperback was published July 7, 2021.

BAST IN SPACE

In *The Intergalactic Empire of Wakanda*, Bast and the orishas are accused of leaving Wakanda for the Intergalactic Empire. The fanatics in the empire offer a greater devotion than Bast's followers on Earth, satiating her needs.

When T'Challa awakens as an enslaved person in this intergalactic empire, he is discovered by Maroons, an homage to the formerly enslaved who launched free rebel societies during enslavement in the Americas. T'Challa is in a world where his Earthly home is a myth, as are the legacies of his peers, of whom many of the Galactic Wakandans are named after. His nemesis is Emperor N'Djaka, named after Killmonger, who has attained the Black Panther status. T'Challa rescues Bast from N'Djaka, but the ferocious orisha is now an impetuous young girl. N'Djaka has seemingly absorbed her powers.

Bast is a true brat. T'Challa has no patience for her teasing and indifferent manner, which he reads as emotional distance from the calamities he's facing. As his memories are restored and Storm locates the king across the universe, he urges his team on Earth to help end slavery in the Wakandan Empire. T'Challa blames Bast's indifference for the challenges back home and the rising tide of tyranny in the Empire.

In this series, the panther goddess takes on the role of Esu, also known as Eshua and Eleggba. Esu is an Ifa,

Santerian, Candobleam, and Vodun deity, sometimes syncretized with Jesus. He is "the one who opens the way," but sometimes also acts as a trickster figure. "Esu is one of the 'functionaries' of Olodumare and is simply out to try to test the human heart," said Gonzàlez-Wippler in *Santería: The Religion*. "As Eleggua, he is the essence of potentiality; as Elegba, he is the wielder of power; and as Eshu, he is the eternal wanderer moving with the swiftness of Mercury from place to place, and appearing where he is least expected," she says.

Bast is more powerful than T'Challa realizes. She charges all of Wakanda's forces with energy, teleporting the Crew and the Avengers, to help T'Challa take down the emperor. A reinvigorated Emperor N'Jadaka, now in the form of philosopher, Changamire, teleports with them, bringing the battle to a head. Bast tricks the emperor, distracting him, and breaks the spear of Bashenga, a nod to the Zulu's adapted short spear fighting style, and hands it to T'Challa, who lands the final blow. "Did you think I did not hear you? Did you think I did not understand?" Bast asked T'Challa.

When Emperor N'Djaka is ultimately defeated, Bast merges with Zenzi, the Nigandan leader and head of a rebel

The first appearance of the spear of Bashenga, as seen in *Black Panther* #7, published January 1978.

Artwork from the cover of *Black Panther* #4, published July 2016.

force seeking Wakandan democracy. Zenzi has her own gifts and was a survivor of Killmonger's super villain campaigns. Both Bast and Zenzi are purposely prodding T'Challa. In their own ways, both the goddess and the woman are forcing him to step into a new understanding of his leadership and responsibilities. Bast wants him to lead a Wakanda that can't become a dictatorship in the future and Zenzi pushes him to allow Wakanda to become a democracy.

"Although his actions may be difficult to understand at times, Eleggua never acts irrationally. It is simply that he knows things that nobody else knows, and always acts according to his own invariably perfect judgment," Gonzàlez-Wippler writes in *Santería*. Much like Eleggba, Bast had a purpose: to ensure T'Challa is the ruler Wakanda needs. Upon his arrival, T'Challa was so struck with the empire's technological achievements that he didn't realize there was an enslaved population laboring in vibranium miles and as servants, some of whom were indigenous to the galaxies. Wakandans had become the unthinkable, a colonizer. Bast reminds T'Challa that this two-thousand-year-old empire was founded on a mission into space that he sponsored in hopes of finding more vibranium. Bast prods an annoyed

T'Challa, and he finally recognizes her power, his role in the injustice, and the responsibility of the collective in upholding a healthy society. "Within African Diasporic religions, you have a path and you're doing the work," said Kinitra Brooks, Leslie Endowed Chair in Literary Studies at Michigan State University. "You're being chastised by your ancestors or the orishas so you can stay on your path and live in your highest potential and rise to your highest being. You can choose not to follow your path and deal with the consequences, but you have a path."

This mythic tale is part hero fantasy, part Esu/Eleggua morality tale, with a reminder about one's larger responsibility to humanity. Trickster Bast prods her avatar, T'Challa, through a journey that makes him an emperor worthy of the responsibility. Then she's reborn, rebooted, and refreshed with doubters and the Wakandan orishas as her witness, rebirthed for a new generation.

MAN AS MYTH

When T'Challa arrives in Intergalactic Wakanda, he becomes a living myth, a man who walks into an empire founded by the astronauts he sent into other galaxies two thousand years ago. The arrival of the true T'Challa has biblical parallels. T'Challa's deeper realization that he is a myth comes at the point where he's lost his memory and is enslaved. Although he arrives as a celebrated king, when he's enslaved, it's the realization that he's a myth that powers his ascent.

The walking myth as epiphany brings free jazz pioneer Sun Ra to mind. Sun Ra, too, both created a myth, claiming

Sun Ra performs in Ann Arbor, Michigan, on September 23, 1978.

Sun Ra posing on the Golden Gate Bridge in San Francisco, California, in 1974.

the Place. "You don't exist in this society. If you did, your people wouldn't be seeking equal rights. I do not come to you as a reality, I come to you as the myth because that is what Black people are: myths. I came from a dream that the Black man dreamed long ago. I'm actually a presence sent to you by your ancestors." T'Challa doesn't exist in the eyes of the Wakandan Empire either until he steps into his name and remembers who he is. In the film, Sun Ra recruits people to fly in his spaceship to the Alter Destiny, a free space of being, whose description hovers somewhere between Wakanda and Djalia, the ancestor plane.

Sun Ra called his practice Myth Science, sometimes calling his Arkestra the same moniker. However, Sun Ra's reference to myth isn't always myth as it's commonly defined. Thomas Stanley, a friend of the jazz legend and a music scholar, said in his book *The Execution of Sun Ra*, "Where the myth and the virtual converge, we find Sun Ra as ontological frontiersman offering his body as a time-stretched filament of possibility connecting here and now into some preferable sub-region of the greater omniverse."

Like Sun Ra, T'Challa also stands at the crossroads of fiction and truth. In the Intergalactic Empire, T'Challa has the glaring revelation that he's a myth within a myth. In the aftermath of his victory, he wonders which story will be told, a pondering that cuts through the fourth wall, that thin veil between character and reader. T'Challa is cognizant of the readers and writers who will carry on his tale, and he is the myth that Sun Ra asserts we all are.

the name of the Egyptian deity Ra, and professed that the underserved were myths as well. "I'm not real, I'm just like you," he told a group of teens in the film *Space Is*

THE ALTER DESTINY

"Science fiction is the ladder upon which today's dreams climb into tomorrow's realities. Alter Destiny is at the top of the ladder."

—Thomas Stanley, *The Execution of Sun Ra*

Jazz legend Sun Ra spoke often of the Alter Destiny, an unfettered space of universal harmony. He named a song after his popular concept and dedicated most of his musical work to ushering it into being. The Alter Destiny was both a destination to reach for and a presence to manifest, both the height of humanity and full creativity, a space where tech and mysticism aligned, and freedom was a state of being. Wakanda as Afrofuturist space and the Alter Destiny have some similarities.

"I think Sun Ra's 'Afrofuture' was Alter Destiny," Stanley writes in *The Execution of Sun Ra*. "This is where it gets trippy. I think Alter Destiny is a 'when' that constitutes a 'where.' Sun Ra says Space is the Place, but where's the place? The place becomes apparent as soon as we get to the time, and the time is up to us."

Sun Ra devoted his work to the establishment of the Alter Destiny, seeing it less as an imagined space and more of an existing one.

"Imagine everything else that we can do above what we've already done," said Stanley, on the Alter Destiny. "All of those things are in reach once we click those gears and get into the time that's right here, but we're not aware. Alter Destiny is in the world, but we can't see it yet."

Sun Ra performing at the Montreux Jazz Festival in Switzerland in July 1976.

THE SIXTH ELEMENT

Writer Kieron Bryant proposed that comics be the "sixth element" of hip-hop. Hip-hop has five elements: deejaying, MCing, dance, graffiti, and knowledge. Bryant reasoned that so many hip-hop artists took on the iconography of super heroes and rapped about their journeys of overcoming, that it should be considered. "From Big

Chuck D of Public Enemy performs as part of Prophets of Rage in London on November 13, 2017.

Hank's Superman references on hip-hop's first chart-topping single 'Rapper's Delight' to Onyx rapper Sticky Fingaz playing Blade in the vampiric antihero TV series, to 50 Cent adapting his *New York Times* best-seller *The 50th Law* into a graphic novel, hip-hop and comic books have been inseparable for over 40 years," Bryant writes on *Djbooth.net.*

"Naturally, hip-hop's founding generation was drawn to the idea that ordinary people could survive trauma and gain extraordinary abilities. In super hero comic books, everyday men and women conceal their true identities in favor of saving their city as an alter-ego in a colorful costume, a reality not dissimilar to that of young b-boys and

b-girls rocking colorful tracksuits to empower themselves in the middle of an unforgiving post-Vietnam War Bronx," Bryant continued.

Oddly, Black Panther isn't referenced much in early hip-hop. Reginald Hudlin compared T'Challa to Public Enemy's Chuck D, though the overlap wasn't immediately obvious. Chuck D is an iconic activist-minded rapper and T'Challa is a super hero and a king. But there are parallels. Chuck D was a straightforward hip-hop artist who spoke truth to power. He spoke as a poet of the people in the name of elevating social consciousness and challenged unjust systems. In 2021, Public Enemy's classic song "Fight the Power" was ranked as number 2 in *Rolling Stone's* 500 Greatest Songs of All Time—second only to Aretha Franklin's "Respect"—while their album, *It Takes a Nation of Millions to Hold Us Back*, was ranked among *Rolling Stone's* Top 5 rap albums. Chuck D's rap style is in-your-face, confrontational social commentary over some of the most innovative sampling and production in hip-hop history (thank you, Bomb Squad and Hank Shocklee). In retrospect, few were bold enough to say what Public Enemy rapped on record.

It could have been Wakanda that Public Enemy was talking about with their 1990 album *Fear of a Black*

Public Enemy in London in 1987.

Planet. However, T'Challa isn't simply speaking truth to power. He's a man of action. He's fearless. As an emissary of Bast, and a symbol for his people, he *is* the power. He's also the system, or at least has inherited a Wakandan form of governance that circumvented others intent on the nation's subjugation. T'Challa's fighting style is clear, concise, bold, and unrelenting, much like Chuck D's poetics, yet it has the flair and grandiosity of the Bomb Squad's dramatic bass, James Brown's electric funk samples, and bombastic horns.

Both Chuck D and T'Challa speak with royal authority. Both men have even-keeled, composed personas to mask their passion. Both have a clear relationship to their own spirituality and cultural legacy. Both men dislike inequality and use their talents and positions to alleviate it. Both men wear black and avoid the glam associated with their status. Both men are comfortable in their own skin.

Nevertheless, early hip-hop's mix of science, mysticism, and poetics were very Wakandan. Many early hip-hop fans were also fans of the Panther, with even more connecting with the story today.

The process of mythmaking in hip-hop echoes both Sun Ra and T'Challa's battles. DJs, taggers, and rappers take on symbol-laden names and alter-egos to step into greatness, just as enslaved T'Challa had to step into his own name and Panther lore in *The Intergalactic Empire of Wakanda* to claim his. This notion of the historically resilient seeking mythmaking and creating avatars is also Afrofuturist, and a part of the Sun Ra legacy. Moreover, "remembering," particularly remembering one's name or where one comes from, is a folk nod to the knowledge stripped away from a person, knowledge that one must forever be in search of if they descend from the enslaved or colonized. Although everyone can't "remember" the names of those lost in the slave trade, they can remember the ancestors and the lessons from the past.

What we call myths today were once religions, with all the expected ceremony and faith. Thor and his adventures, the Roman gods and their authority, or the Celtic fairies were all spiritual practices, and we now mostly share them as tales (although there are people who acknowledge all of these deities today). We look to these myths as great storytelling or the essence of human values on the path. In other cases, these myths are populated by real people whose stories stand the test of time.

Modern myths, like Black Panther, carry values too. In an era where people increasingly rely on tech to communicate or social lives go virtual, the modern myth is a heartfelt reminder of humanity and possibility. Sun Ra often shared his beliefs in poetry. "We hold this myth to be potential," Sun Ra writes in the poem of the same title. "Not self-evident but equational, another Dimension, of another kind of Living Life."

FROM UNDER THE SHADOWS

This infusion of contemporary myth and spirituality into the Black Panther mythos normalizes African/African Diasporic storytelling devices and the otherworldly in pop culture. It also normalizes more open discussions about themes in African spirituality among those who felt they should only discuss it in secret. "The word 'hoodoo,' however, was seldom spoken by African Americans," says hoodoo practitioner and author Stephanie Rose Bird in her book *Sticks, Stones, Roots, and Bones.* "They did not really want to name or recognize this eclectic collection of African holdovers that endured and reminded us of the Middle Passage and slavery." She adds, "The word 'hoodoo' was never spoken in my home, yet its tenets were evident in my upbringing."

For much of the twentieth century, African spirituality was demonized. Vodun was maligned in pop culture.

Other faiths were either dismissed as foolhardy or not referenced at all. Although various faiths were mentioned in the works of Toni Morrison, Ntozake Shange, filmmaker Julie Dash, and others, it was widely unpopular to have wholistic references in comics. The apprehension around African religions, even among some Black audiences, was high. "These are organized religions," said Brooks of these beliefs. "They manifest differently than Abrahamic religions, but they are no less complex, and no less theorized." More Black churches in the US are acknowledging the African practices that inspired their faith or actively adopting practices in worship. Those curious about the ideas in African and African-derived practices can even run across these ideas in comic books.

The woven world of Wakanda helps readers understand the philosophical ideas at play, and can act as a starting point for further learning. "I have a PhD and I'm knowledgeable about all these things, but in the religion I'm a baby," said Brooks. "I think that folks don't always want to recognize the discipline and the hierarchies that exist in the religion and that it takes work to be a part of it." Ultimately, she says, your ancestors will lead you to someone who is helpful and who wants you to be your best self, just as T'Challa routinely finds support from Bast and the other orishas that make up the Wakandan pantheon.

After T'Challa gains the title of emperor, and another chastisement from Bast, Storm reminds him that the story of the change they brought will be retold forever. "They're going to tell stories about this, T'Challa," said Storm. "You and I will be faded and there will still be stories." "Yes, but which one will they tell, beloved?" T'Challa asks. Storm

replies, "The one about the king who wanted to be a hero and the hero who was taken as a slave, and the slave who advanced into legend." They will tell all of these stories, with the orishas and Bast threaded throughout.

Storm of the X-Men in cover art by Salvador Larroca for *Black* Panther #34, published February 2008.

THE NEXT RENDITION

When the Hartsfield-Jackson Airport in Atlanta posted flight times to Wakanda when the film was released in 2018, travelers may have laughed at the idea of buying tickets to the fictional city. But those who speculated about what Wakanda looked like may soon have one place that brings it to life.

In 2020, officials of the Ghanian Cape Coast, the African Diaspora Development Institute, and several local companies committed to the creation of the city of Wakanda in Ghana. The city is designated as a pilgrimage for people of African descent to learn the continent's history and culture. Wakanda will include a university, teaching hospital, and resorts, among its civic institutions. Perhaps most importantly, it's an imagined space taking form.

In a statement, the collective said, "The African Diaspora is committed to change the African narrative and strongly feel that a united African Diaspora can bring the capacity that is needed to move Africa to its rightful place on the world state."

The announcement came a year after Ghana celebrated The Year of Return, a year of activities to commemorate 400 years since Africans were sold into slavery in what would become the United States. The return was a larger project to encourage people of African descent in the Americas to think of Ghana as a second home, a nation to invest in, visit, and build with. Ghana was among the African nations that regained its independence in the 1950s, a movement that shaped T'Challa's creation. Whether the city resembles the story it honors or not, what's most exciting is that it seeks to capture the spirit of home that Black Panther inspires.

STORYTELLERS ALIGN

Black Panther has invigorated the public imagination around African/African Diasporic possibilities. There's a growing demand to experience Wakanda and the creative visions the world invokes. The Wakandan world was a global reminder that all too many didn't know the cultures of

Africa, hadn't experienced the full range of Black creativity, and simply yearned for more—more stories, worlds, and realms of the imagined.

There's something gripping about seeing how transformative a story like Black Panther can be. The hole T'Challa's story fills—and the absence felt when the Panther myth was lesser known—is glaringly obvious. Although the wave of works in the African/African Diasporic fantastic

A Funko Pop figurine of Shuri.

A Black Panther action figure at Toy Fair 2019 in London.

can't all be attributed to Black Panther's success, the rise of T'Challa's mythos served as a social juggernaut. Black Panther's elevated reach in recent years gave some the confidence to tell stories, and others the confidence to bring them to light.

"People are looking for answers, looking for things that make them think," said Bill Campbell, founder of Rosarium Publishing. Black Panther made the conversation about Afrofuturist works easier. The divides revealed by the protests in 2020 unveiled how essential diverse speculative works are in educating the wider public.

People are demanding new spaces to challenge what the future can be. They seek out fresh stories to keep them galvanized, enriching stories that can transport them from one worldview to another, and tales that keep them uplifted in the face of adversity. Black Panther has shed light on a floodgate of stories, old and new, from Black cultures. Creatives who once toiled under the radar, criticized for creating worlds enmeshed in the African fantastic, are rising into the light. Books, comics, TV shows, and films are budding with Afrofuturist ideas, and Black Panther fans—and a bevy of devoted creatives—have themselves, in part, to thank for it.

Stories from Black cultural lore of the fantastic are having a golden age. Tomi Adeyemi's *Children of Blood and Bone*, the first of the Legacy of Orisha novel series, sold over a half million copies before it was acquired by Paramount Pictures for development in 2018. The story involves a magical quest centered on the world of the orisha. *Yasuke*, a Netflix anime loosely based on the true story of Japan's legendary Black samurai, from creator/director LeSean Thomas, featured a soundtrack by Flying Lotus and voice-over by actor LaKeith Stanfield. Black Sands Entertainment launched a Kickstarter campaign to garner interest in their comic book *Black Sands: The Seven Kingdoms*. Egyptian god Ausar leads this tale, and readers follow his rise in Ancient Egypt. In 2022, the company attracted investment from billionaire Mark Cuban and comedian Kevin Hart on the TV show *Shark Tank*. Disney announced the production of *Kizazi Moto: Generation Fire*, an animated anthology of African futures.

Disney is also producing the feature-length animation *Iwájú*, in partnership with Kugali. Founded by Nigerian writer Ziki Nelson, Kugali first came to prominence with a crowdsourcing campaign in 2018, after beginning as a comic anthology. "There isn't a single question we're trying to answer, but rather a household conversation we want to continue," Nelson said at the campaign's launch. "How do we Africans see ourselves and our respective cultures? What is it like to live in Lagos, Harare, or Nairobi? What would our myths and legends look like visually? These are some of the driving factors behind Kugali."

He added, "After all, despite growing up in Nigeria, I grew up reading American comics and Japanese manga. These stories have always been an endless source of joy and inspiration to me. There's no reason why

A Lego minifigure of the Black Panther.

Kugali can't provide that same experience for comic book readers across the world."

The adaptation of the comic book *Naomi*, created by Brian Michael Bendis along with writers David Walker and Jamal Campbell, is part of the wave the *Black Panther* film helped facilitate. *Naomi*, adapted by Ava DuVernay, was helmed by actress Kaci Walfall, who plays a teen discovering her super powers. The relaunch of a host of comic book titles with Black super heroes can be credited to Black Panther's astonishing success in the last decade as well. *Bitter Root,* a comic that follows a family in 1920s Harlem fighting supernatural forces, also written by Walker and Chuck Brown with illustrator Sanford Greene, was acquired for TV adaptation. African/African Diasporic anthologies, including *Africa Risen*, edited by Sheree Renée Thomas, Oghenechovwe Donald Ekpeki, and Zelda Knight; novels like *Raybearer* by Jordan Ifueko, in which the protagonist becomes a royal goddess; and graphic novels like *Hardears*, a Barbadian story of super heroes in the Crop Over Festival, are continuations of the Black Panther effect. *Harriet Tubman: Demon Slayer*, a reimagining of the abolitionist as vampire killer as graphic novel is in adaptation. TV or film adaptations of books by Octavia Butler, N.K. Jemisin, and Black Panther writer Nnedi Okorafor are also in the works. These stories center women in worlds that keep audiences spellbound.

"One of the things I love the most about *Raybearer* is that so many stories about Black girls in particular, especially dark-skinned Black girls, their coming of age always has to do with their abuse and being disempowered and having to rise from that or heal from that," said Jordan Ifueko, the novel's author, in a virtual book talk for Charis Books. "While those stories are important—I really wanted a story where the conflict comes from the power that she has already and what

she decides to do with that inherit power. She has power within, she has power given to her from this empire, and she can choose to cling to the small bit of privilege that this empire gives her and protect that—or she can risk even that and bring about the world that she knows needs to be."

Black Panther has shifted the needle on representation in comics and fantasy. Stories that center empowered Black characters in marvelous worlds are flourishing, and the wave of stories will continue, in all formats. Moreover, Black Panther's impression on the public has galvanized stories from other cultural pantheons shaped by Indigenous, Latinx, Asian, and queer writers in the US and abroad.

Black Panther has inspired STEM curriculum, culture clubs, reading groups, world-building games, and models for new futures. The character and his adventures have prompted interest in African histories, liberation histories, Black legends, African spirituality, and Afrofuturism. Black Panther's stories present a model for feminism, leadership, and teamwork. The Panther has spawned creativity as far-ranging as a Wakandan cookbook and ethical platforms for asteroid mining. Books on the Panther Effect, the film's impact, and how one can be a Dora Milaje are all testaments to the Panther's grip.

"I definitely felt a combination of pressure and pride," said Nyanyika Banda, the writer and chef who created *The Official Wakanda Cookbook*, in her interview with *BlackEnterprise.com*. Banda studied the comic and devised some seventy recipes to reflect the culture. "The lore of Black Panther and what Wakanda means now socially is so important, not just for Black Americans but to people of African descent around the world." Banda, a woman of Malawi American heritage, pulled recipes from her knowledge of African cuisine and family cooking, so even the cookbook spoke to a pan-African synthesis.

A LOVE STORY

Black Panther has contributed to the Black speculative fictions that push storytelling to new heights. Black Panther, as modern myth, is highly Afrofuturist. In many ways, Afrofuturism in its latest iteration is having its own intimate conversation with Black Panther, the mythos and the worldview forever informing one another, as the tide of legendary stories skyrockets. The imagination comes alive in Afrofuturist storytelling. There are ways of thinking about space, time, innovation, and liberation that can facilitate living happier, healthier lives that emanate from the creativity of the African continent and Diaspora. Black Panther has come to be an example, and in some cases a barometer, for what that world and its power dynamics look like.

Perhaps the imaginative qualities that bloom after reading *Black Panther* will always have a place in the hearts of those who read it, fanning the flame for future creatives and visionaries alike. Though the Panther's legend is fairly new, its roots are ancient and mystifying. There are legacy fans of Black Panther who never thought they'd see the myth as resounding as it is today, as new fans grow up never knowing a world without the Panther's omnipresence in pop culture.

Black Panther fans can't talk about Panther lore without a tinge of excitement, as they see that glimmer of a world realized, a world they know in their hearts to be true. Black Panther is affirming, complex, and wondrous. May the Black Panther mythos be a constellation in a celestial world of stories to come. May the best of what Wakanda has to offer come alive for those who crave the legend's wisdom.

Artwork by Mark Brooks for a *Black Panther* #1 variant cover, published April 2016.

ACKNOWLEDGMENTS

My gratitude to those who've supported this work is overflowing.

I thank John Jennings for his graciousness and insight.

I thank Karama Horne for her thoughtfulness.

Special gratitude to First Aid Comics for being a beacon in the comics shop world and always having copies of *Black Panther* on hand that I needed for my research.

Special thanks to Third Coast Comics and Terry Gant for their generous support.

Thanks to all who agreed to be interviewed for this book. Their colorful memories of their Black Panther delights are forever endearing.

Thanks to all the creatives who've shaped the Black Panther narrative, one that lives on in hearts and minds.

Thanks to Marcellus Womack for his recommendations.

Thanks to editors David Wohl and Katie McGuire, photo researcher Alison Muff, copy editor Helena Caldon, and proofreader Karen Levy for their hard work and dedication to this project.

Thanks to Rage Kindelsperger for her support.

Thanks to my dynamic literary agent, Jessica Papin.

Thanks to Delia Greve for bringing this project my way.

Thanks to my family, my dad Lloyd, my mom Yvonne and stepfather Phillip, my sister Veronica, and the awesome ones, Simeon, Adonis, and Mecca, for their enduring support.

ABOUT THE AUTHOR

Ytasha L. Womack is an award-winning author, director, independent scholar, and dance therapist. Her book *Afrofuturism: The World of Black Sci-Fi & Fantasy Culture* was a 2014 Locus Awards Nonfiction Finalist. She lectures on Afrofuturism and the imagination for audiences around the world and was a cocurator of Carnegie Hall's Afrofuturism Festival, a nationwide arts festival, in 2022. Her other works include the sci-fi novel *Rayla 2212*; the Kickstarter project *A Spaceship in Bronzeville*; and nonfiction books *Post Black* and *Beats Rhymes and Life: What We Love & Hate About Hip-Hop*. Her films include the Afrofuturist dance film *A Love Letter to the Ancestors from Chicago* (director) and *Couples Night* (screenwriter). Ytasha was an inaugural resident for Black Rock Senegal, helmed by artist Kehende Wiley in Dakar, showcasing her zine *Liquid* at the 2022 Dakar Biennial. Other residencies include serving as writer-in-residence at the WOW Festival in Liverpool, Kickstarter, and Emerson College. She's featured in the Smithsonian documentary *Afrofuturism: An Origin Story* and contributed essays to the National Museum of African American History and Culture's Afrofuturism exhibit companion book, *Afrofuturism: A History of Black Futures*. Her short story, "Liquid Twilight," is featured in the anthology *Africa Risen*. Ytasha has a BA from Clark Atlanta University and is an alumnus of Columbia College in Chicago. A Chicago native, Ytasha can be found dancing to house music and drinking unusual amounts of tea.

SOURCES

Araujo, Ana Lucia and Preston Blier Suzanne "What the 'Woman King' gets Wrong and Right About the Dahomey Warriors." *The Washington Post*, 20 September 2020, www.washingtonpost.com/made-by-history/2022/09/20/what-woman-king-gets-wrong-right-about-dahomeys-warriors/.

Berkowitz, Lana. "For Storm and Black Panther It's My Big Fat Superhero Wedding." *Chron* 22, February 2006, www.chron.com/life/article/For-Storm-and-Black-Panther-it-s-my-big-fat-1875027.php.

Berry, LaSonya. "Effective Leadership: What Black Panther Teaches Us About Being A Leader." diversityprofessional.com/effective-leadership-what-black-panther-teaches-us-about-being-a-leader/.

Betancourt, David. "Ta-Nehisi Coates Took Black Panther to Dark Places and It Paid Off." *Washington Post*, 29 May 2021, www.washingtonpost.com/arts-entertainment/2021/05/29/ta-nehisi-coates-black-panther/.

"Black Panther Brings Afrofuturism to the Big Screen." *Radio Open Source with Christopher Lydon, 90.9 WBUR*. 1 March 2018, https://radioopensource.org/the-world-of-wakanda/#.

"'Black Panther' has Public Enemy and a 2005 Comic to Thank for His Theatrical Debut." MTV News, 13 February 2018, www.mtv.com/news/pphgne/reginald-hudlin-black-panther-interview.

Bockhaven, Vicky van. "Leopard-men of the Congo in Literature and Popular Imagination." *Sci Elo South Africa*. January 2009, www.scielo.org.za/scielo.php?script=sci_arttext&pid=S0041-476X2009000100006.

Brooks, Nicholas. "[Spoiler] Has Finally Left the Avengers- But Were They Ever Really a Right Fit." *CRB*, 23 April 2022, www.cbr.com/avengers-black-panther-chairmen/.

Burrard-Lucas, Will. "Black Leopard: My Elusive Quest to Photograph the Most Elusive Cat in Africa." *Will Burrard-Lucas Photography Blog*, 11 February 2019, blog.burrard-lucas.com/2019/02/black-leopard-in-africa/.

Byatt, Kieron. "How Comic Books Became the 6th Element of Hip Hop." *DJ Booth*, 23 April 2019, https://djbooth.net/features/2019-04-23-comic-books-sixth-element-of-hip-hop.

Chamber, Catherine. *Myths of Ancient Egypt: Gods and Pharoahs, Creation and the Afterlife*. Amber Books, 2019.

Cunningham, Joel. "The B&N Podcast: Reginald Hudlin on the Black Panther." *B&N Reads*. www.barnesandnoble.com/blog/sci-fi-fantasy/bn-podcast-reginald-hudlin-black-panther/.

Cush, Lincoln. "The Women Behind the Black Panther Party Logo." *Design Observer*. 1 February 2018, designobserver.com/feature/the-women-behind-the-black-panther-party-logo/39755.

Dash, Mike. "Dahomey's Women Warriors." *Smithsonian Magazine*, 23 September 2011, https://www.smithsonianmag.com/history/dahomeys-women-warriors-88286072/.

Daut, Marlene. "Inside the Kingdom of Haiti: The Wakanda of the Western Hemisphere." *The Conversation*, 23 January 2019, theconversation.com/inside-the-kingdom-of-haiti-the-wakanda-of-the-western-hemisphere 108250#:~:text=The%20fictional%20kingdom%20has%20a,black%20state%20in%20the%20Americas.

"DMC From Run DMC on the Power of the Black Panther – RIP Chadwick Boseman." *Double Down News*, 3 September 2020, www.youtube.com/watch?v=8x81LcytRXA.

Eldredge, Richard L. "That Time Black Panther Came to Georgia and Kicked Ku Klux Klan Ass!" *Eldridge ATL*, 16 February 2018, www.eldredgeatl.com/2018/02/16/that-time-black-panther-came-to-georgia-and-kicked-ku-klux-klan-ass/.

File, Nate. "Summoning Freedom." *Boston Review*, 17 August 2022, www.bostonreview.net/articles/summoning-freedom/.

Francisco, Eric. "'Black Panther' Writer Unpacks His Sci Fi Film Debut and Upcoming Marvel Comic." *Inverse*. 17 October 2021, www.inverse.com/entertainment/john-ridley-needle-in-a-timestack-interview-black-panther.

Gallaway, Lauren. "Black Panther and Storm – A History of Their Marriage & Why It's Important." *Fandom*, 15 January 2018, www.fandom.com/articles/black-panther-storm-married.

Gay, Roxane. "The Letter From the Editor." *Inverse*, 19 October 2021, https://www.inverse.com/entertainment/roxane-gay-superhero-issue.

Gonzelez, Migene. *Santeria: The Religion.*, 2nd Ed, Lewellyn Publications, 2020.

Grand, Alex and Jim Thompson. "Don McGregor Biographical Interview" *Comic Book Historians*, 3 May 2020, comicbookhistorians.com/don-mcgregor-road-to-black-panther/.

Groth, Gary. "Jack Kirby Interview." *The Comics Journal*. 23 May 2011. www.tcj.com/jack-kirby-interview/6/.

Hance, Jeremy. "In the Kingdom of the Black Panther." *Mongabay*. 15 January 2013, news.mongabay.com/2013/01/in-the-kingdom-of-the-black-panther/.

Harding, Xavier. "Black Panther Has the Coolest Tech in the Marvel Universe." *Xavier Harding*. 10 May 2019, www.xavierharding.com/read/wakanda.

Heil, Emily. "In the New Wakanda Cookbook, Black Panther Food Lore Comes to Life." *The Washington Post*, 12 April 2022, www.washingtonpost.com/food/2022/04/12/wakanda-cookbook-black-panther-recipes/.

Isaak, Joshua. "Marvel Fixed Black Panther by Ignoring His Original Comic Title." *Screen Rant*, 13 December 2021, screenrant.com/marvel-fixed-black-panther-jungle-action-comics-wakanda/.

Joho, Jess. "Danai Gurira on How 'Black Panther' Challenges the Conventions of Femininity." *Mashable*, 22 February 2018, mashable.com/article/danai-gurira-interview-black-panther-okoye-beauty-female-power.

"Katt Williams: Full Interview with Arsenio Hall:Netflix is a Joke: The Festival." *Netflix is A Joke*, 5 May 2022, https://www.youtube.com/watch?v=NxnGDoJAXns.

King Jr, Martin Luther. *Strength to Love*, Beacon Press, 2019.

"Lowndes County Freedom Party." Digital SNCC Gateway, snccdigital.org/inside-sncc/alliances-relationships/lcfp/.

Lumumba, Patrice. *Congo, My Country*. Praeger, 1962.

MacNamee, Ollie. "Previewing John Ridley and Juann Cabals 'Black Panther' #1 From Marvel." *ComicCon*, 21 November 2021, www.comicon.com/2021/11/21/previewing-john-ridley-and-juann-cabals-black-panther-1-from-marvel/.

Magnett, Chase."Interview: Christopher Priest Talks 'Black Panther' and His Focus on Character."*Comicbook*, 17 February 2021, comicbook.com/marvel/news/black-panther-christopher-priest-movie-interview/.

Manseau, Paul. "The Surprising Religious Backstory of Black Panther's Wakanda." *The Washington Post*, 7 March 2018, www.washingtonpost.com/news/acts-of-faith/wp/2018/03/07/the-surprising-religious-backstory-of-black-panthers-wakanda/.

Martin, Michileen. "The Untold Truth of Black Panther." *Looper*, 14 September 2020, https://www.looper.com/246588/the-untold-truth-of-black-panther/#:~:text=Likewise%2C%20Lee%20said%20he%20conceived,mindful%20of%20going%20against%20stereotypes.

McCann, Jim. "Divining the Design." *Black Panther: The Complete Collection* by Reginald Hudlin, 2017.

McGregor, Don. "To Follow the Track of the Great Cat With Renewed Wonder on His Panther's Quest." *Black Panther: Panther's Quest*, March 2018.

Morse, Ben. "Writer Reginald Hudlin Asks and Answers the Question: "Who is the Black Panther." *Marvel*, 31 March 2020, https://www.marvel.com/articles/comics/writer-reginald-hudlin-asks-and-answers-the-question-who-is-the-black-panther.

Myers, Maddy. "Brian Stelfreeze on Illustrating the New Black Panther Series & Working with Ta-Nehisi Coates." *The Mary Sue*, 3 October 2015, https://www.themarysue.com/brian-stelfreeze-black-panther/.

Narcisse, Evan. "'The Miracle is Wakanda' Ta-Nehisi Coates Says." *Polygon*, 26 May 2021, www.polygon.com/interviews/22454722/black-panther-comics-ending-ta-nehisi-coates-interview.

"The Original Black Panthers Fought in the 761st Tank Battalion During WWII" *History*. 11 April 2018, https://www.history.com/news/761st-tank-battalion-black-panthers-liberators-battle-of-the-bulge.

Park, Andrea. "Black Panther Fans Can Now Fly To Wakanda From Atlanta." *Conde Nast Traveler*, 21 February 2018, www.cntraveler.com/story/atlanta-airport-wakanda.

"Redempter: Jordan Ifueko in Conversation with Ytasha L. Womack." Charis Books & More, 20 August 2021, www.charisbooksandmore.com/event/redemptor-jordan-ifueko-conversation-ytasha-l-womack.

Riesman, Abraham Josephine. "How an Untested Young Comics Writer Revolutionized Black Panther." *Vulture*, 16 February 2018, www.vulture.com/2018/02/don-mcgregor-panthers-rage-black-panther.html.

Roff, Col. Cherie. "Marvel's Black Panther Sets the Tone for Leaders Everywhere." *Air Force*, 4 April 2018, www.af.mil/News/Commentaries/Display/Article/1484364/marvels-black-panther-sets-the-tone-for-leaders-everywhere/.

Rosebird, Stephanie Rose. *Sticks, Stones, Roots and Bones: Hoodoo, Mojo, and Conjuring with Herbs*. Llewellyn Publications, 2004.

Some, Malidoma Patrice. *The Healing Wisdom of Africa*. Jeremy P. Tacher/Putnam, 1998.

Space is the Place. Directed by John Coney. 1974. www.criterionchannel.com/space-is-the-place.

Stanley, Thomas. *The Execution of Sun Ra*, Wasteland Press, 2014.

Tonar, Remington and Talto Ellis. "Wisdom From Wakanda: Five Transportation Insights From 'Black Panther.'" *Forbes*, 27 May 2018. www.forbes.com/sites/ellistalton/2018/05/07/wisdom-from-wakanda-five-transportation-insights-from-black-panther/?sh=3ae24337264e.

Wilson, Claire. "Wild Black Leopard Photographed in Africa for First Time in 100 Years." *The New Scientist*, 13 February 2019, www.newscientist.com/article/2193803-wild-black-leopard-photographed-in-africa-for-first-time-in-100-years/.

Womack, Ytasha. *Afrofuturism: The World of Black Sci-Fi & Fantasy Culture*. Lawrence Hill/Chicago Review Press, 2013.

"The Woman King Gina Prince Bythewood to Direct Viola Davis in Film on Dahomey Amazon Warriors" *Shadow and Act*, 14 July 2020 shadowandact.com/the-woman-king-gina-prince-bythewood-to-direct-viola-davis-in-film-on-dahomey-amazon-warriors.

"World of Black Heroes: Reginald Hudlin Interview." *World of Black Heroes*. *Hudlin Entertainment*. hudlinentertainment.com/world-of-black-heroes-reginald-hudlin-interview/.

Yanes, Nicolas. "Kwame Mbalia and Prince Joel Makonnen Discuss Their Novel, 'Last Gate of the Emperor,' and Ethiopian Culture." Scifipulse.net, 1 May 2021, https://www.scifipulse.net/kwame-mbalia-and-prince-joel-makonnen-discuss-their-novel-last-gate-of-the-emperor-and-ethiopian-culture/.

Yekaterina, Barbash. "Cats, Bastet, and the Workship of Feline Gods." *American Research Center in Egypt*. www.arce.org/resource/cats-bastet-and-worship-feline-gods.

IMAGE CREDITS

Every effort has been made to trace copyright holders. If any unintentional omission has been made, Epic Ink, as an imprint of The Quarto Group, would be pleased to add appropriate acknowledgments in future editions.

Unless otherwise noted below, all images are copyright to Marvel.

Page 82 (right) Joa Souza/Dreamstime

Page 83 (top) Alvin C. Krupnick Co, photographer. Retrieved from the Library of Congress.

Page 83 (bottom) Alvin C. Krupnick Co, photographer. Retrieved from the Library of Congress.

Page 84 Janusz Pieńkowski/Alamy Stock Photo

Page 85 Jimlop collection/Alamy Stock Photo

Page 86 (left) Emma McIntyre/Getty Images

Page 86 (right) Jimlop Collection/Alamy Stock Photo

Page 87 Gargolas/iStock/Getty Images

Page 88 Tomas Abad/ Alamy Stock Photo

Page 89 (left) Redtea/iStock/Getty Images

Page 89 (right) Interfoto/Travel/Alamy Stock Photo

Page 91 Scherl/Süddeutsche Zeitung Photo/Alamy Stock Photo

Page 92 Thomas Cockrem/Alamy Stock Photo

Page 93 MPI/Stringer/Getty Images

Page 94 Kirn Vintage Stock/Alamy Stock Photo

Page 95 Science History Images/Alamy Stock Photo

Page 96 Shareif Ziyadat/Getty Images

Page 108 John Sciulli/Getty Images

Page 110 CPA Media Pte Ltd/Pictures From History/Alamy Stock Photo

Page 111 Photo Researchers/Getty Images

Page 112 CPA Media Pte Ltd/Pictures From History/Alamy Stock Photo

Page 113 Bettmann/Getty Images

Page 114 Interfoto/History/Alamy Stock Photo

Page 115 Pictorial Press Ltd/Alamy Stock Photo

Page 118 Boaz Rottem/Alamy Stock Photo

Page 119 Sihasakprachum/iStock Editorial/Getty Images

Page 120 Paul Bruinooge/Patrick McMullan/Getty Images

Page 122 Ray Tang/Shutterstock

Page 123 Suzi Pratt/Getty Images

Page 124 Geisler-Fotopress GmbH/Tony King/Alamy Stock Photo

Page 125 Frederic J. Brown/AFP via Getty Images

Page128 Alpha Historica/Alamy Stock Photo

Page 130 Jessica Rinaldi/The Boston Globe via Getty Images

Page 131 Frazer Harrison/Getty Images

Page 132 Bettmann/Getty Images

Page 133 Everett Collection Inc/Alamy Stock Photo

Page 134 Gallo Images/Getty Images

Page 135 Louise Gubb/Corbis via Getty Images

Page 146 UPI Photo/A.J. Sisco/Alamy Stock Photo

Page 147 (left) Artokoloro/Alamy Stock Photo

Page 147 (right) MCLA Collection/Alamy Stock Photo

Page 148 Helene Rogers/Art Directors & TRIP/Alamy Stock Photo

Page 149 Science History Images/Alamy Stock Photo

Page 153 Leni Sinclair/Michael Ochs Archives/Getty Images

Page 154 Jim McCrary/Redferns/Getty Images

Page 155 Andrew Putler/Redferns/Getty Images

Page 156 Ollie Millington/WireImage/Getty Images

Page 157 David Corio/Michael Ochs Archives/Getty Images

Page 161 Craig Russell/Alamy Stock Photo

Page 162 Peter Hogan/Alamy Live News/Alamy Stock Photo

Page 163 Wirestock, Inc./Alamy Stock Photo

INDEX

Page numbers in **bold** indicate illustrations

S

T

U

V

W

X

Y